1. Allen Ginsberg
2. Anne Buchanan
3. Philip Whalen
4. Charley Plymell
5. Neal Cassady
6. Dave Haselwood
7. Justin Hein
8. Maggie Harms
9. Glenn Todd
10. Maia Harms

The Book of Friends

*Scenes from Life on Gough Street
from a 1963 Journal*

◊

by Glenn Todd

with an afterword by Charles Plymell

Bottle of Smoke Press
New York

The Book of Friends—Scenes from Life on Gough Street

The Book of Friends © 2017 by Glenn Todd

"My Last Days at the Gough Street Flat" © 2017 by Charles Plymell

"November 23, 1963: Alone" Excerpt © 2017 Harper Collins, used by permission.

Photo on pages 79 : Justin, Maggie, Maia, & Glenn in Mexico

Photo on page 81: Charley Plymell and Glenn Todd in 2011

All Rights Reserved

Cover design by Bill Roberts and Phil Scalia

First Printing

ISBN-13: 978-1-937073-70-1

Bottle of Smoke Press
Post Office Box 66
Wallkill, NY 12589
orders@bospress.net

Excerpts from Nov. 23, 1963: Alone
by Allen Ginsberg

Alone
...
with Charley muttering in his underwear strewn bedroom
with Neal running down the hall shouting about the ractetrack
with Ann with her white boys ass silent under the Cupid thigh
with Lucille talking to herself, feeding the pregnant cat Alice
with Anne mourning her pockmarked womb & the hard muscled chest of her Lover
with David's red wine fireplace casting shadows back to the Duchess farmboy
    faggot of Wichita, on fire in mainstreet
with Alan with horses teeth metafysiks demurely insisting he was intensely
    so over coffee
with Glen o'the lisp & Justin the olding bluejacketed man love off in autos
    to Mexico cactus hope
with the fat lady with babe in the auto, feeding & grieving her adolescence's
    backseat
with Robert in his black jacket & tie deciding to make a point of his courtesy
    over the kitchen linoleum
...

When I reported my typewriter stolen, the policeman who came politely and carefully asked me questions and wrote my answers down. "House tended to in absence by friends," he noted. To me: "Definitely an inside job. Who are the suspects?"

I murmured negatively, but your name, Dan Rowan, sounded my heart like a gong, yet I could not say it. I could see too well the scene: you rousted in some endpad of despair in the hopeless grey fog of San Francisco, among other lost denizens listlessly crawling the floors, last night's wino-heaven and pill-paradise crashing down to the dead hell of morning. The fuzz at the door, where you always suspected they would be. Busted. Eeling your way out of this one. After they have gone, feeling the high triumph of escape, hating me all the way across town dialing the police from the Blue Room, seeing suddenly the dullkill looks in the eyes of zombie friends, wondering if this means the end of that scene, which you have also always known would happen, clawing immediately for wine dregs or the ragged fluff of a Velo inhaler, ready to zonk out again. Out of it—to anywhere but Here, this victim life that reduces you to genuine dramatic tears of resentment. Or off to the tank for a couple of days to a nightmare scene of down. You who were meant to be smothered in flashbulbs and spotlights, projected in technicolor onto America's heart, facing the insidious mirror of now like an aging movie queen, "How much longer can I make it? Is it over?", suddenly laughing with hideous Dracula glamor, knowing that it will never end as long as it can get worse. Let's get high, honey, and I mean high.

* * *

Dave Moe is back in town. Comes up to us in Foster's Cafeteria, Charley, Justin, and me, where we stand in line for coffee, and begins to talk. Our energyless aftermath of pot doesn't stand a chance against the zigzag leaping of his words. He is not so far gone as I remember. I listen carefully, trying to follow, because his face is so handsome to look at. When his thoughts are too much trouble to make sense out of, I watch his eyes. He is a tall blond man in his early twenties with perfect features and horn-rimmed glasses. His most beautiful attribute is his coloring: rose-milky-gold. A tiny indentation marks one of his cheeks.

Moe talks compulsively and not quite incoherently. He has just come back from Los Angeles. He tells us of being arrested there for standing in the middle of the freeway, of his "rare bird" disguises, of practices of L.A. police on the prowl, of courts of law, of white-collar attitudes toward humanity ("They stand in high buildings and look down and watch the insectitude."), of labor practices among the braceros in the San Joaquin Valley. He leaps from subject to subject, his mind making strange parallels, sometimes interesting, sometimes odd, often merely a complex way of stating the obvious. When he makes a point that particularly pleases or disturbs him, he begins to stutter, his face lights up and falls apart in laughter. It is then he looks his most beautiful. For a moment words fail him but beauty succeeds.

Charley Plymell makes several attempts to say something back—we all do—but there is no real communication. It becomes a drag. He is just enough in contact that we can't laugh at him without feeling he'd notice.

A uniformed guard stands at the doorway of Foster's when we enter. Charley, with his eye out for such things, remarks as we pass, "Oh, oh, Foster's has police now." We haven't been there an hour when the guard swoops down upon us, acne-scarred and quiveringly righteous. He seizes upon Moe, telling him that if we don't order something we will have to leave. Poor Moe protests that we have already ordered. The guard looks significantly at Moe's empty place. So we leave, Charley muttering that it is almost here, that it is almost happening, that they are having to place guards around to keep us under control, they are so frightened.

Off to the midnight corner of Polk and Sutter. Justin cuts for home, tired, highhair and hornrims above ghostpale boybeauty. Tomorrow the skid-row drag of job. . . .

We wander to Maggie's to look for Haselwood but he's out. Maggie comes forth sleepily from her bedroom, hair down, looking round and young and naked under her short robe, comes out not entirely unhappy—glad to see someone at the end drag of an evening without people—but soon brought down by Moe, who sits down at the white kitchen table and begins a fast hard monologue. Maggie with her woman-sense digs the straight of things and doesn't dig Moe particularly, who she senses wants an impersonal stopover in whatever pad with something sitting in front of him that breathes. Moe detects audience withdrawal and talks faster and faster.

We cut, Charley to bed "to write a few things", and Moe and I to Fillmore Street. Moe is strangely silent now, holding himself in check but leaning slightly forward, waiting to let me have my say so he can know what to talk about. Comes on straight and quite friendly; we talk about Negroes and Fillmore Street. I talk about Negroes but can see he doesn't dig or understand my stories, which he turns into causes for the unfortunate. I point out those heavy wires hung on telephone poles along the street, the black cloud that hangs over Fillmore on the brightest of days. Sideglancing I sum up Moe. Only his face is beautiful, his body is large, shapeless, and sexless under baggy clothing, his hands soft and round like a Scandinavian girl's. I want him to be completely crazy so it will free me of involvement. I want to ask him about all the stories I have heard about him, like letting animals out of the zoo and digging up corpses, but I can't. I sense the hunger for a friendly scene in him but I am wary of his reputation.

"Would you like to smoke some grass, man?" I ask on upper Fillmore. Sometimes the jargon fits my tongue awkwardly as a rubber sheath. I do not ask him if he wants to turn on; once I did that with McClure and he looked cool and said, "To what?"

He says, "Yeah," with cautious enthusiasm and suggests his pad, which is a few doors away. His room is neat and clean and I am a little surprised. A bookcase of books, a sagging bed, a white oilcloth kitchen table, a burner to cook on hidden in a corner.

He watches me closely while I am rolling a joint, but I am watching a cockroach run across the kitchen table. He swats the roach.

"Cockroaches don't bug me," I say; then remembering once when I went into a pitch-black room and the light was turned on, I heard a continuous rattling, like a paper sack shaken, from the cockroaches running to escape, I add, "Unless there are just too fucking many."

"Man, they do me," he cries and runs around the room with a newspaper, swatting.

His room is at the front of the second floor and has four large windows across it. We sit in front of them and turn on. Neon glows up at me from out of the fog-covered city, long Fillmore Street and west coast Negro scene. I feel an urban melancholy take over and numb my head. Moe is looking at me but I can't say anything. I feel he wants a hipper scene with nightlong jabbering. I don't quite trust him and am afraid to get too friendly.

The joint is now a roach of another kind, which I refuse. He sticks a needle through it, holds it before his mouth and draws and draws until there is only a tiny charred ash left, no larger than the head of a pin. We laugh at it affectionately.

"I haven't had any in a long time," he says hesitantly.

"You want to smoke another?" I ask, and roll a second joint. I put it on the oilcloth of the table, white on white.

I look at his books, many of which I have read. Plutarch's Lives, Keats and Shelley, Jane Eyre, Hegel, Hume, lots of good books. I come on sincere. I talk about books, houses, rent. He comes on sincere and cautious. I am sad, we can't get going. We talk about scenes, rooms we have lived in.

"'I have lived in rooms, rooms, rooms,'" I quote. "Do you know that poem?"

"Lamantia," he says. "I've looked at it."

We sit. "I've got to go," I say. I look at the joint. "I'll lay this on you, if you like." It's Justin's pot.

"I sure could use it. Thanks a lot." He sounds awkward. He asks for my address and I give it to him without hesitation but with a buzzing sound of doubt in my head. Then I'm gone.

On to dark Fillmore out of my brains in the wee hours of night, holding. I quicken my pace as I hear footsteps behind, and suddenly I feel like a chorus boy in my tight black pants and expensive sweater. I laugh and shake a nostalgic hip at the past, going home.

The house on Gough Street is an anachronism. Tides of city planning have swept around it, but left it primly intact in all its Victorianism. Stucco apartment buildings, small businesses have it hemmed in. The street in front is busy and one-way. A couple of blocks away the gaudy specter of the Jack Tar Hotel raises its dull moderne bulk. Countless beatnik-hipster scenes have filled the Gough Street pad, then drained away, leaving its walls ringed with the sad evidence of their passing. Nervous, hung-up ghosts flit from room to room. Remnants of meth electrify the air, mists of marijuana have cooled its rafters; immobility of junk has settled in its corners, sometimes so thick you could heat it in a spoon. It has an immediate history that stretches back into the great Beat days of the fifties when Allen Ginsberg, Peter Orlovsky, and Robert LaVigne lived there, and a vague legend that reaches back to the forties, and even the thirties, a gapped lurching toward the present in intertwining and overlapping plots. Everyone has a Gough Street story: I once attended a someyear New Year's Eve party there, a pall of despair festooned with balloons and crepe-paper streamer.

Maggie with her big round body and her long dark hair and her baby, Maia, live in third story, the top flat, or at least half the top flat. A curtain in the hallway divides her flat in two, leaving the front part to the noises of strangers yelling and flushing toilets, and we don't know what's going on in there and we don't care.

Haselwood, a young publisher of "avant-garde" poetry, has a room with Maggie. He and Maggie don't make it together, but they make it, each finding something of home in the other, enough to keep it pleasant most of the time. On the wall above her round kitchen table Maggie has tacked a sign carefully lettered in orange Crayola: I AM RESPONSIBLE. Across the room another sign proclaims LSD DID, to which someone has added, NOT; which someone else extended, HING; a final flourish completes the sign with A LOT. "LSD DID NOTHING A LOT."

The landlord, almost non-existent, occupies the ground-floor flat, an unobtrusive, let-me-alone individual that nobody ever seems to see. Sandwiched between is Charley Plymell's flat, a many-scened and ghost-haunted territory that he currently shares with Pat, a tall bewildered girl with a face that turns successively from fashion model to blonde Egyptian princess to poor little witch girl to pale asylum inmate. They don't make it together either. She is one of Charley's people, an army that stretches endlessly back, whom he brought recently from Kansas, abandoned in sink-or-swing San Francisco, took up again when he looked across the debris of rejection and saw in her eyes hurt grappling for clearer vision, nearly dead hope struggling for a foothold on the crumbling mountain of Sanity. She saw in him momentary tolerance and accepted it. Now they live together in brother-sister truce, waving with caution a white flag of concern.

Charley is at the end of a long soul-killing love affair. His sunny blonde swinging girl has left him for the joys of Julliard and cello, using a knife on an unborn part of him before leaving. The rooms he sits in now were decorated only a few months ago prior to her joining him from the wheat-harvesting Midwest, golden with the promise of increase. In a burst of Charley-swing, he made ready the rooms of love. Justin painted the door, a vision of high joy exploding, rising suns of orange and gold, and the word LOVE! across it all in magnificence aflame. On a tall ladder Haselwood painted the angels of the alcove gold, and the alcove itself blue with leftover paint from mine and Justin's Blue Room on Delmar Street. Maggie suggested Day-Glo pinkish-orange for the strip of picture molding, with highlights added around the room. A tall mirror in a Day-Glo frame reflected the whole scene. It was Charley's pop-art room, the longed-for carnival of his heart come true.

But it did not work. Now it is a shrine to aborted love. A quieter, darker mirror has replaced the one of Day-Glo, and a worn Persian carpet hangs on the wall to hide some of the more unbearable excesses of color. Four Cheracol bottles sit on the fireplace mantel, holding tall white candles. Charley sits before the fire, sipping Cheracol and listening to hillbilly songs while reading the sonnets of Shakespeare. All meanings and implications of words unite within his brain: Shakespeare and hillbilly intertwine. "Shakespeare's sonnets are like country songs," he tells me.

"How like the winter hath my absence been from thee," he sings in quavering country twang. I am convinced enough to join him in a duet. Harmonizing voices: "What old December's bareness everywhere!"

※

"Hello, how're you," says Haselwood, greeting Marian, as she walks in on a quiet Friday night scene. A Big Sur poet's child is six months within her body, making it solid and matronly and huffingly protesting. Faded littlegirl blonde beauty glows wanly from her face.

"Terrible," she said, bringing the whole down world in with her. Seeing her expression, Charley shuffles momentarily in the doorway and cuts for downstairs.

"Gee I hope I didn't bug Charley out of his place."

"No," says Haselwood. "He's been trying to get us to go out all evening. I think he wants to make a North Beach scene or something."

Marian is insistently verbal. She talks rapidly and listens alertly. Every group she enters immediately bears her imprint. Soon she is off, her hands dancing delicately in the air to punctuate her sentences. Her current scene—pregnancy, new apartment, job—she sketches quickly with Marian-logic and analysis, adding deft moral quips and chuckling asides. She is a strange California transplant from Boston puritanism—an especially disturbing mirror we look into uneasily, reflecting as it does the guilt of our collective and individual ways. In Marian's fall we sinned all. She is reproachful as an unflattering photograph that we fear shows our looks exactly.

"I wish I had some of those magic crystals that makes the fire burn different colors," says Haselwood during a lull. "Maybe we could experiment, salt or soda or something," says Maggie.

"No, I want something to make the fire burn green."

"Try some pineapple rind or banana peel," I say, referring to a camping incident in which Haselwood had thrown pineapple rinds on the fire, stinking and smoking everything up.

Marian listens intently to the mention of a scene she didn't make, always feeling left out, making me feel I left her out.

"We could throw you on the fire, Glenn," Haselwood says to me. "What color would you burn?"

"Smudge," I say. "The color of smudge, and I would cover everyone with a greasy film and you couldn't wash me off."

"That's your dream of glory, isn't it, Glenn?" says Marian with her little laugh. "To smear yourself over everyone about an inch thick and nobody would be able to wash you off."

"No, Marian," I say. "Just over those who would burn me alive."

Haselwood gives a wicked, conciliatory chuckle.

Justin cuts.

Later I find Justin and Charley downstairs reading Ecclesiastes. They are hung up on a certain verse, laughing and asking, What does it mean? A typical Charley excursion. He loves to pursue words to the point of inanity, where they make no sense at all, then smile in triumphant discovery at the world.

"Ask Glenn what it means," he says to Justin, and disappears to the kitchen.

Justin looks at me resentfully, thinking I have followed him down from upstairs to break in on his swinging scene. He does not hand the Bible to me.

Two can play.

"Shades of Sister Geneva," I say. "Isn't that a King James version you're holding? I didn't know Catholics were allowed to read that."

Charley returns with a joint and a sonnet, both of which he hands to me. Charley is a poet, but unlike some poets, also works. I mean he has a real job in the real world. Or do I mean the opposite?

SONNET

The Lord of Chance has loosed his planet beads,
As Thee alone, in vast decanter wane,
That time reveals a morning-glory seed

To sweet the hour of Thy daring pain.
No longer hopeless charter memory hold
Tarot hand that spreads the stars array
But as flowers to adorning sun unfold;
The Sun loves Thee, as Thou the seed must play.
Though fear and hate have taken more than few,
As if their names were pressed into a tomb,
We must with lips that kiss the morning dew
Sing like Nature, when in her private room.
      So subject caught in King Self's dying net.
      At Nature's door we could at least be met.

It is a beautiful sonnet, but a little complicated for me, zonked as I am on pot.

Justin hands me the Bible. The verse in question reads: "For there is a man whose labour is with wisdom, and with knowledge, and with skillfulness; yet to that man that hath not laboured therein shall he leave it for his portion. That is also vanity and a great evil."

"Well," I say, "probably what is giving you trouble is the 'shall he leave it for his portion' part. I think it is a matter of syntax."

"Yeah, that's where it gets funny," Charley says.

"I think it means that he shall leave the portion of wisdom and knowledge that he worked for to a man who hasn't worked for it, which is also a form of vanity." I don't think I'm right, I just want to say something.

We talk about Ecclesiastes, whether it is upbeat, downbeat, or merely the exact drone of a man saying this is the way it is.

"It doesn't exactly cheer me up," I say.

"It's not exactly a drag either," says Charley.

"Is that the way it is?" asks Justin.

"Having a stag party, I see," says Haselwood from the doorway.

Justin gets defensive, and the guilt from leaving Maggie and Marian upstairs falls down upon us all. Haselwood feels exempt because he was the last to leave, Justin the guiltiest because he was the first to break the established scene. No one wants to talk about

Marian, but we do, endlessly analyzing and re-analyzing her motives.

"I don't like to cut women out of the scene," Haselwood comes on. "There is a real earth connection there that I like, something very real. You miss a great deal if you cut it out. I enjoy being around women."

"You have a right as a human being to walk away from whatever bugs you," Justin comes back. Right now he's got a bad thing for Marian. The argument goes on and on, until I go upstairs to invite the women down. It's too late. Marian has cut and Maggie is in bed with a stomach ache.

It's also too late to go home, so Justin and I flop in the blue alcove under the gold guardian angels. Outside, the wheels of traffic on Gough are like the sound of rain, sheets of steady driving rain, big city song lulling me to sleep.

At nine o'clock the next morning the clock radio pops on with rock-and-roll whinebeat, asking me if I feel like crying, like crying, like crying. It's too early to live but Charley is up with Justin. They're going to take LSD, a small hit because that's all they have, then go to the de Young museum and look at Art. They are peering down the avenue of the coming day with uneasy eyes of anticipation. Everything is slowly gathering to the jitters and I want out of it.

"Charley," I call. "You've got to give me something if I have to get up. I haven't had enough sleep."

He slips apart a plastic capsule of Dexedrine and pours a few dozen yellow and green grains on my tongue. Little tiny jawbreakers in the mouth of a giant.

It's enough to get me up and soon I'm swinging through a breakfast of grapes, cantaloupe, and coffee. I'm cleaning the Cheracol shrine furiously, making it bright and sunny and hip in the Saturday morning light, sweeping and emptying ashes from the fireplace. One can only go so far in cleaning the Charley chaos before incurring the Charley ire, so instead of giving everything the scrubbing I desire, I compromise and clean a good-sized circle in the middle of the room.

Then upstairs with glossy energy and goodwill (I don't want

to watch them take the LSD) to Haselwood and Maggie at their breakfast table. They are young and tender, refreshed after the night's sleep. Haselwood is wearing a wool shirt with an open collar and a white T-shirt. His face glows with the translucent beauty of an angel, clear blue eyes framed an oval of brown beard. Then downstairs again to Charley's where they have made it and are waiting.

"Pat," calls Charley.

"Yes," says Pat, tall luminosity appearing in the doorway.

"Do you want to go to the museum with us?"

"Yes," says Pat.

It's off to the de Young by bus and a walk through the residential streets of San Francisco. I can see the LSD working in Justin and Charley, not too strong yet but there, confusion and blankness taking hold of the facial muscles. Charley is tasting himself. A man is washing a car, a child is playing with a skate. I wonder what Charley and Justin are seeing, what mad extensions of logic and behavior they are making of the simple actions.

Into the green of Golden Gate Park. I take out a joint and blow up. It's a cool spacious world with only a few LSD nerve-endings. A man with a dog walks by. The dog chases a squirrel.

Justin draws in his breath. Charley says, "It looks to me like society could at least keep its cruel dogs off the animals of the park." The man looks strangely at him but goes on.

I stand before a bright tree that is covered with red blossoms like silk tassels or rare birds, and it blows me away. Justin and Pat walk ahead. She is tall and he is small and they are smiling evenly at each other.

Charley lies down in the path and feeds sunflower seeds to the squirrels. "Look, they know just how to crack them open and get the goody." Passersby eye him distrustfully but without much curiosity. We walk the winding lanes of Golden Gate Park. The day is sunny but a chill wind pushes us on. At the foot of the statue of Goethe handing the laurel wreath to Schiller, we find Pat and Justin talking. The cool innocence of children fills the clear air of Saturday morning.

The de Young doesn't make it. I move rapidly from room to

room, looking at my favorite paintings briefly, "Doing your frantic thing," Justin says. A heavy, depressive air emanates from the dark browns and golds of the religious paintings. Madonnas smile benignly but smugly, holding up misshapen Baby Jesuses; weirdly proportioned cherubs lift coy eyes to heaven; crucified Christs spurt streams of blood in perfect arcs over frozen figures; annunciatory angels, looking ready to attack, break in on a solitary Virgin. I look to the still figures and upright penises on red-and-black Greek vases: I grapple with the centuries.

Vibrancy possesses Justin, his flesh is almost visibly rippling. "Let's go to the Legion of Honor. This place is awful. There's a Tintoretto out there that is really joyful, really beautiful, bursting with light."

Outside on the steps we are hung up. The idea of catching a bus to another place is more than Charley can bear. Woe and discomfort inform every muscle and limb. "Surely we could get a ride with someone," he says loudly and pointedly to the people passing by. "Surely there is someone going to the Legion of Honor." He looks at each person. "We could hire a car. Pardon me, sir," he says to a boy whose face is aflame with acne. "Do you have a car?" The boy doesn't even break his stride and shakes his head no. "Pardon me, miss," to a young girl in Bermuda shorts, "do you have a car?" "No, I don't," she says, looking back over her shoulder to a girl friend, giving her impatient hurry-up signals. Charley will not be put off, he wants to stop one of the cars going by, he wants to hire the man who is washing his car, he wants a taxi.

Pat and I look at each other and smile inanely.

"It's some kind of human contact he wants to make, some kind of easy thing he thinks should be going on between people," Justin explains to us. Charley is stricken with immobility. It is labor for him to put one foot in front of the other. I know that it is because he thinks the LSD has failed, he is not completely prostrate, he is disappointed that some conscious control remains. The rest of the day will be downhill with only tag-ends of revelations. But he is on with Justin, and Justin wants to go to the Legion of Honor, so we go. The story is the same—nothing makes it. We wander through sunny rooms of rosy-grey pouting court ladies. Still, they look more accessible than movie stars. Thighs and bosoms push roundly into reality. The Tintoretto fails Justin, but not completely. He looks at it for a long time. It is a Madonna with Child, warm-fleshed figures in the foreground, lovingly painted. The real attraction for him is a sunrise that is bursting forth in the corner of the work, flooding the canvas with still, gold light.

"Art just doesn't go far enough," he says.

There is an organ recital they want to attend. I wait outside, lying on the stone railing overlooking Golden Gate point. The hills of Marin are late-summer gold and brown: the bay is dumbstriking blue, with a few whitecaps: sailboats are venturing out far past the bridge today. I am bound to this beauty by the stone railing, but my never-quiet mind is haranguing with itself, so the still scene is not mine to possess, distant yet flat against my eyes. I wish to put my hands forward and rend it, as if it were a painted cloth that hides another view.

***

North Beach and the American Saturday night. People are everywhere; the bars are full and spilling out on the street. All the nightclubs have queues in front of them. We pass places where Negro rock-and-rollers gyrate and moan and claw the air, where Arabian belly dancers fresh from L.A. twirl their tasseled asses, where folksingers with guitars and stomping feet pound the world. Everywhere everyone sits entranced. But it is a slick scene, a money scene, a scene of senseless energy and dull delights. I can find no place in it—the high-heeled bouffant girls of careful makeup and the bland ivy-leagued young men are from another world, this world, the world that belongs to them, the square American world doing its American thing, its thing that will go down in history beside the Greek thing, the Roman thing. Isolated, I admire and deplore its energy coupled with assurance. Where did it lose me along the way?

"It is good to see the young heart poundeth still and the young brain turneth on," sings Charley, lover of American youth.

We settle for a small club with African music and dancers,

where the cover charge is too high, the drinks too expensive, and I complain to the waitress so she won't bug us for another round during the show. The show is billed as African, but the Negroes are obviously American, except maybe for the leader of the troupe, who announces he is from Angola or Liberia or Nyasaland, I don't know, mysterious worlds of negritude. He wears an odd purple lamé robe and sings or beats drums with great flourishes, purple sleeves flopping, accompanied by a half-dozen other musicians. The rhythms are insistent and enlivening, so gradually we warm up to the performance. Suddenly the dancers are on stage, three women and two men. The women are the color of dark honey, small but with large hips and big bellies. The men are darker, very thin, with every muscle showing beneath taut skin. The dancers are swift, leaping and twirling and pounding, urgent but not frantic, sexual but never lewd. I am transported to another place, where these golden people dance in festivals of praise beneath blue sky and bright sun; where bodies sing hosanna to the flesh they are captured in, hymns to the grace of being, songs for the earth world.

We're back on the streets headed for Market, Justin is singing a little song to the sides of buildings, snapping his fingers. I cock a careful ear to catch the words. "High joyous," he is singing, "high joyous and joy, joy, joy."

On three a.m. Make It Street, all the unfortunates are out, never too late to Make It. Twisted faces cruise past, grim arrows flying toward unknown targets. Mostly loser queers who have found no one, hips too fat or heads too small, too old, too ugly, too strange to even vaguely fit anyone's fantasied ideal of the American male. A hermaphroditic queen goes by, lurching forward awkwardly in cowboy highheels, his wide hips jerking; a broad carved leather belt proclaims his name to the world. He gives me a bold/timid look from thick lenses and bobbing Stetson, and a wavering (Make It!) crooked smile. I smile back but quickly look away.

Standing next to us at the bus stop are three young hustlers, all under age. They are short and bounding and pudgy. Blond heads jerk amidst gestures and exclamations. They are coming on to a sharply dressed man in his late thirties, who stands sexy and pert in front of them.

"Nine and a half," screams the handsomest of the three,

"and I'll give it to you right here on Market Street!" The man laughs and digs him in the ribs with a friendly jeer. He smooths off toward the penny arcades with a busy wave.

"That's Al," the boy explains to his companions. "Good for ten, and a nice guy. Good God, look who's coming."

Out of the night swoops a rare bird. At first I think it is a greasy ugly fat girl, but then I see it's some far-out queen, out of his mad head. He is wearing black skin-tight pants or leotards, and his hips are round and his knees close together. A black V-necked sweater with the sleeves pushed up to the elbow. Under the dark wool his tits are jiggling. At his throat gleams a seed-pearl necklace with a tiny gold cross. His hair is brushed high up into the night, as near to bouffant as he can get it. His face is huge and round, the eyes and the mouth large. He has smeared pancake makeup across his face thickly, his eyes are carelessly and heavily made-up. He is not wearing lipstick but his lips are pink and alive in the smear of his face. The eyes are in control, burning and open to the world. Around his shoulders is a raincoat, which he opens and closes to reveal as much or as little as he cares to. A crazy nervous companion is at his side, hopping and flitting in attendance like a sparrow.

He glides up to the hustler, whom he obviously knows, wrinkles his nose and gives a coy and satisfied "Hi!"

"My God, the police will drag you in if they see you like that," the hustler says with a note of genuine awe in his voice.

"Not if I see them first!" the queen answers, tossing a mad flirtatious glance, eyes prospecting for attention. "I wanted some Saturday night fun," he says, looking for a moment directly into the hustler's eyes. "I thought I'd come out and see what I could stir up."

"Yeah," says the hustler, "You come out thinking you look like a girl and you've got a dick hanging down there showing through those tight pants."

"Maybe I do," says the queen in a quiet voice, and stops very still and looks into space, blanking herself out, the way perhaps small animals do when they feel a hawk flying over. But in a moment or two he is himself again, pulling at his sweater and fixing his cow-like adoring eyes on the hustler and he's warming up. Soon he's off again into the night, cynosure of tired eyes of Market, strangers glad to have someone to make them smile through the debris of a cyclone civilization.

I am thinking of a golden people dancing by firelight under close bright stars.

※

Pat. Poor little Pat. Except that Pat is not little. She is tall. And thin. Fashion model thin, Egyptian thin. She sits in on many of our scenes. Does she listen? She speaks only when spoken to.

"Pat," says Charley.

"Yes," says Pat.

"Sometimes when you're looking at people's faces do they change into something else before your eyes?"

"Yes," says Pat.

Charley: "Man, she's on LSD all the time."

"Pat," says Haselwood.

"Yes," says Pat.

"When you smoke pot, do you get high? I mean do you experience things differently?"

"Yes," says Pat.

What does she see? Night after night, she sits silently. Every time anyone looks into her face, there is a communication so intense and clear that it is unbearable for more than one harrowing second. Sometimes the communication is dazzling pain, sometimes it is distilled laughter—whatever it is it is so immediate that no one dares it very often. What judgment does she pass upon us all? Is she bored? Is she shocked? Is she some far-flung priestess wise beyond our ways, letting us fret at her feet like children? Once, she sought answers as she looked from face to face in succession, over and over. Now, she sits and stares into space. Every so often she shakes her head violently, as if to erase some unwanted revelation, as if to certify the reality of what she sees. What is it she is seeing?

Pat is never cruel, although sometimes blunt, and she always speaks the truth. I see her as a lonely bewildered girl, almost done in by an unloving, unimaginative nation.

Pat is a painter. She paints ethereal childlike scenes of

mystère. Graceful naked girls dance in blue air under a silver moon. Beautiful white-magic ladies stare out from night-enchanted places. All the women are her.

Thinking of this and wanting to thaw my cold, hip heart, I say to Doug, the friend of lonely ladies: "I would like to be friends with Pat, but I don't know quite how. And I am afraid."

Doug's laughter originates in a world that veers madly out of control when he feels discomfort. "So would I," he says, laughing that laugh. "But what I am afraid of is that if I became her friend, I would just about be her only friend."

"Yeah."

*
**

Justin and I sail into Charley's flat through the back door past the kitchen table where Pat is sitting listening to Moe's machine-gun monologue, through to Charley's room.

"Oh, oh," says Charley, catching sight of me. "Glenn's been working overtime."

Charley has a new girl, who has been around for a few days now, a little brown creature in a little brown dress, and now she scurries for cover like a little furry animal shyly bounding for its nest.

"What's happened, Charley," I say swiftly, "is that we're being evicted and we wonder if we could move in here."

"Yeah, sure," says Charley. I love him for making quick decision based on love.

I am wound up and have to run down before I can stop. I will repaint the living room, erase the Cheracol shrine, along with the tidemarks of other drifting scenes, frightened in my heart at the prospect of what could become an awful situation, telling myself I am strong, I can do it, I can do it, I can transform this pad, make it swing with right life, bugged and intrigued with visions of the new, feeling myself coming on too strong, boring everybody, but fixing my determination at a bright level even though no one cares. Paint it green, paint it brown, paint it sky-blue, knowing this is evidence of my squareness, everyone else just moves into places; then not caring, fuck them all, I ramrod it through, trying frantically to make things right in my head, apologizing.

And facing the issue of Charley.

Like all intelligent and creative people, Charley can never be categorized. Not that I aim for boxes as my mind tosses forth opinions. But people do fall into patterns of behavior, and some of Charley's actions cut disastrous swaths through people who get in the way of his careless shears. I am not afraid of him. I find him far too interesting to give him up because I might get too close.

I am comforted, somewhat comforted, by the fact that Charley also faces the issue of me. What does he think of me? Does he think I will try to make him? I know that he respects me, and in friendship love and respect go hand in hand. I feel a ruthless compulsion growing in me to sweep aside all that gets in my way.

"Is it all right with you if we move in, Pat?" I ask.

"What about the back room?"

"We won't be using it. You'll still have a place to paint."

"Okay," says Pat.

It's all settled. Settled. Settled. I guess. We'll move in at the first of the month. I guess.

※

"The dining room has ghosts," says Charley. "Some people that used to live here kept it locked up all the time. When Marian lived here it was her room and she was the only one that would even dare go in it."

"Then we'll exorcise the ghosts."

Haselwood enters the dining room holding high the battered remnants of a palmetto fan and a smoking dish of crystals of frankincense. Maggie, Justin, Charley, and I follow, ringing elephant bells.

I am trying to put Haselwood on. I feel a tinge of malice. I want him to do some wild incantation and chase the ghosts from the room, really flip out, so that I can throw it at him like a dart in some future date when he is ballooning through the spheres of intellectuality. He senses my game and will not play. It gets harder to fool Haselwood every day.

"We never did give that costume party," someone says. "We ought to give it as soon as we get the place fixed up."

"A costume freak party," Haselwood corrects. "That way everyone can get just as far out as they want to. We could invite all the Market Street costume freaks."

"Oh, oh," says Charley. "We could invite the North Beach Negro girl with the funny cloak and the patches and squares of colors."

"And the bobbie-sox girl with the white-satin hairbow."

"And the pinhead."

"I think we ought to invite the pirate," says Justin.

"And that guy with the book. He walks up beside you and opens it to some page and looks at you significantly, snaps it shut, walks on, looks back, opens the book, shows it to you, snaps it shut."

"What's the book about?"

"You can never quite remember. It's full of pictures pasted-in, and slogans, and things. Politics. Religion. Art, I think."

"That pinhead," says Charley. The pinhead is one of his favorites. "Man, you don't know what world he's in. He walks around fast as he can with his hands in his pockets, and laughs hee! hee! hee! all the time. I really wonder where he is."

"Maybe they all would think they had come home," Maggie says wistfully.

The talk goes on. People come and go, laughing. Moe suggests characters from Dickens that we could invite.

At the end of the evening Haselwood climbs down from where he has been sitting atop a bureau. "Well, do you think we have properly exorcised the ghosts?" A comfortable expression lights his face.

✻

The little brown girl scurries away again, smiling. I am reminded of the North Beach dancers.

"Charley," I say, "what's your girl's name?"

He looks around to see if she is gone. "I don't know. Lucille, I think. I just call her Cheracol."

"Charley, Charley, Charley," I shake my head, aglow in some mysterious way. "You can't do that."

"Oh, guess what's happened. Pat has lost her cherry."

"What!" I sit stunned, a picture of Pat and Moe sitting at the kitchen table, flashing on and off in my mind like a traffic signal.

"Yeah, last night I passed Pat's room and there was Pat in her gown, standing up, and Moe was down on his knees in front of her kissing her box."

***

I walk through the cold August night, the wind is chill. I am a lone newspaper scooting along the gutter. A woman is standing close to a news vendor, looking him square in the eyes, saying to him almost harshly, "And try to take care of yourself. I don't want to be a widow." And I am sure she doesn't, who does in the empty, blowing night. Long plains of deserted furniture stores, ghost manikins in sale store windows, faint pulses of bars in funeral-blue neon, buzzing faintly like bad snake dreams. I buy a Mr. Goodbar in a liquor store; I smile pathetically at the proprietor; he responds and calls out Goodnight. I sing a sad hillbilly song from long ago, try to fan a sentimental coal of comfort in the dark, but the words are not quite right. Aimless, astray, who wants to be a widow on a night like this, outdone by death and a cold cold wind?

I hold high courts of justice in my brain, where all my actions are vindicated and wept over by black-robed figures of high ideals and fine mentality.

***

When the police called and told me they had found my typewriter in a pawnshop, I felt the teeth of the trap give a little, and hushed a panicky elation in my chest. If I could get it back, I would be outwitting the fates in some small way, one tiny stolen move while no one was looking. Quickly now!

At the pawnshop the dealer won't let it go. "I put out forty dollars on that machine..." he hesitates.

I feel anger rising in me, dragging forth debris from the muddy bottom of frustration. I can see my sweet little machine at arm's length, urging me on. We exchange words.

"See you in court!" I sing out my goodbye.

"Get outta here, I don't want to talk to you!"

I'm like an insect whose nest has been destroyed. I buzz Market Street angrily for fifteen minutes trying to find a pay phone. I call friends for advice; then the public defender. I don't want to pay. The police will do nothing: their job is merely to locate stolen goods.

"Unless there has been an arrest, it is a civil matter," says a lady's harassed voice at the other end of the telephone. "I suggest you try the Legal Aid Society."

The voice at the Legal Aid Society is cool and sexy: "Can you afford an attorney? We don't give advice over the telephone. Come in to see us at one-fifteen."

While waiting for the lunch hour to pass, I order a chocolate malt at the Woolworth fountain. It is thin and watery and too much chocolate. Malts are getting smaller and smaller and higher and higher every day. I look around. Woolworth's is shuddering under a dome of plastic. Plastic is everywhere.

I'm too early. I stand smoking a cigarette with other people waiting in the hall. A funny old dame with short-cropped hair and wearing pointy curly-toed Arabian-night bedroom slippers is talking in a whiny voice to a commiserating man who is wearing behind his glasses pink plastic goggles with tiny holes in them. A big Mexican man is sitting on the floor talking to his wife in low rapid Spanish. They look miserable.

I want to listen to the funny old dame, because she's now talking to me, but I'm so nervous I can't follow her. Her voice and the pink-goggle voice are complaining back and forth. I am reminded of pastoral poems with the sing-song plaints of shepherds and shepherdesses.

"... United Crusade ain't worth a damn...."

"Poor people digging in garbage cans."

"I call it the Starvation Army. . . ."

"City Hall so damn snotty. . . ."

"But the Volunteers of American wouldn't let me go until they were sure my job was steady."

". . . and I said how in the hell can I work if I been sick for a month."

". . . a little advice without all the run-around. . . ."

". . . and when he said all that money people is giving is going into the bigshots' pockets, they cut him off the air! ! ! !"

I'm startled by silence. The old dame is staring at me quizzically.

"You're right," I say. "It's awful."

In the office I meet the sexy voice and she was better on the phone, but I turn on to her utter bewilderment. She's somewhere lost in the law machine. I lie to her about the amount in my bank account, and she gets to me for a two-dollar registration fee.

The waiting room is a drowning pool of woe. The Mexican woman is saying to her husband in nervous Spanish, "It's better if you can't drive, it's better not to know how to drive," and he is blowing a fallen wisp of hair from her forehead and smiling reassuringly. A mournful Negro chick of about sixteen is sitting with a two-year-old boy on her lap. The funny old dame is picking at him and crowing. The kid drops a package of pastel candy wafers and they roll everywhere. Everyone stoops to pick them up. An arch Oriental lady pushes one gingerly out of the aisle with a high high-heel shoe.

I look out the window at the insectitude. I am out there on Market and I have found Dan Rowan. I have struck down his fleeing figure with a mighty blow between the shoulder blades. I am weeping and smashing him in the face, hauling stolen money from his billfold, taking what he owes me and more, screaming, "Desperate slut, you've made a nervous wreck of me!" I'm wondering why I can't relax, after all it's only a matter of forty dollars, which I would gladly pay just to get out of this office. I have an agonizing picture of the irate pawnbroker snapping off the keys of my typewriter one by one.

A bouncing little lawyer sings out my name. He's grinning

like the village idiot, rubbing his hands gleefully together in anticipation of something. As I follow him, the funny old dame clutches my arm as I pass. "Good luck!"

I soon get the lawyer's turn-on: it's salacious stories. I have hardly stated my case until he's off. "Pawnbroker" is the key word. It reminds him of a rape case in which a pawnbroker helped convict the true rapist, not the poor innocent guy who had been identified by the weeping rapee on the witness stand. I am squirming and hardly able to keep from babbling. He is gesticulating and laughing, like the clown of the high school picnic.

". . .and it seems the police couldn't figure out how the guy with just a knife could stand off this big football-player type and rape the girl at the same time and it comes to light that he always chose couples who were in the act, you know—screwing!—and attacked them. Usually they didn't report it because they didn't want to say 'There we were screwing when this guy sticks a knife in my back and . . .' but he went too far this time—shaving the girl's—some sort of sexual uh freaky deviant—shaving the girl's head and putting those leg manacles on her arms. . . ."

Right about there he had me hooked and he knew it. It was the leg manacles that did it.

"So you see, Mr. mmmmuh, everybody's down on the pawnbroker. But they do cooperate with the police and if they didn't you wouldn't have found your typewriter in the first place, and when they start losing too much money, they're going to stop cooperating with the police. So you can take him to court to sue for the typewriter or you can take him to small claims court where there are no lawyers—" and on and on, out of his legal head, following me to the door, getting in juicy details of far-flung, sexually illustrative cases.

"My lawyer," I tell the pawnbroker, "has convinced me that you people do cooperate with the police and that perhaps it is not unfair that I should reimburse you for some of your loss. . . ."

"Now you're talking like a gentleman," he says, and his face radiates kindness, and waves of mollification flow over me.

We settle for twenty-five, and he shows me the signature

on the pawn ticket. I see my name scrawled in tiny nervous script, and it is the same as the one on the card that I am carrying in my pocket, mailed to me from Mexico by Dan Rowan, where I had sent him once to score some pot, a card reading: "YES-S-S-S, but don't shake the beads. Miss Destiny."

Oh, your rareship Destiny Rowan Doll, where are you in the nervous city? That forty couldn't have lasted you long. And why do I feel guilty?

※

Sonnet to Gold

> I leap for final gold—I see its gleam
> Above those sad abandoned flags of shame
> I once held high, like standards of my name.
> Upon the martyr's slope of cross and dream
> Is death, where light vacates the vibrant cells
> That strive in losing battle with the sun.
> I am set free when my own hand rebels.
> The furnace of my blood burns steadily.
> I call no stops nor stoop to see its sheen
> On sprays of love or hatred's folded wing.
> It is the flame beyond anxiety.
> These cells demand their way and I have won
> The torch of final gold I will become.

※

On goes the paint. I am transforming the living room at Gough Street. The ceiling: Parchment White; the walls: Ultra Gold. Charley takes a spray can of metallic gold and gilds the picture molding: under goes the Day-Glo pink. Justin and Haselwood have insisted on brown-ochre for the walls. Haselwood helps me choose it. Charley grabs a brush to test it on the walls. Everyone is horrified. Charley and Lucille do not like it.

"It's the color of baby shit."

Gabble and hiss of criticism. (I will, said the little red hen.)

It's really too late, no one can stop me, because I have fallen in love with the name: Ultra Gold. The Ultra Gold Room. It reminds me of a sonnet I have just written and nothing can make me give it up. But I can't pacify Charley. He is in the throes of some agonized anger that he is momentarily directing toward the color of the paint. I am getting very high-strung painting the ceiling on the rickety old ladder. He doesn't like the funny white of Parchment either. Although it's a Friday, Charley didn't go to work. He's like an inconsolable cat, moving here there everywhere, with everything and nothing claiming his attention. I am thinking he is bugged by our moving in, that I am pushing too hard.

In comes Haselwood of the cool diplomatic head. In a few moments he has consoled Charley and placated me. He puts more paint on the walls. Charley begins to like it and goes to his bedroom.

Haselwood and I are on high shaky ladders for the rest of the afternoon. Once I look out of the windows and see Lucille and Marian Weston in front of the house. Marian is smiling and talking, her hands making delicate spirals and blossoms in the air. At five-thirty Justin leaps breathlessly through a window into the room. Charley comes back just in time to go to the paint store and help me choose a color for the woodwork. Russet.

"I like warm colors," he explains.

It's too late to work anymore. There are no lights in the living room. I have clipped wires to remove an old lighting fixture and inadvertently cut off the electricity for the whole room.

Maggie, Justin, and I wander to Japantown to eat. We sit in a little restaurant eating sashimi and donbury. I look out of the window, which overlooks Geary Street and the vacant blocks of slum-cleared rubble. ("The war of San Francisco," little girl longago Chipmunk once told me, Alice-in-Wonderland leading me, an aching giant, peyote-high, across the weedy trashfilled lots, past concrete steps leading up to the invisible ghosts of Victorian mansions. "The war that nobody is winning.") Lavender fog is moving in swiftly across a charcoal blue sky. Maia, Maggie's baby, is pounding the table with wooden chopsticks and making bubbles out of babytalk and laughter. I am depressed and withdrawn. Will

Gough Street work out? Will Charley turn on me in a swift grownman's arc of childish destruction? Will I, Glenn, be done in?

Later, on the bus going home, a vision of love! I see the rooms of Gough Street filled with music, people move happily through them. Every gesture is a dance of joy. The scene glows in warm, vivid colors.

*
* *

Saturday the room is done. Haselwood, Justin, and I obliterate the ghosts of Gough with paintbrushes and endless cups of coffee supplied by Lucille. Only the blue alcove is left untouched. The sliding doors between Charley's bedroom and the living room are painted white and gold. The whole effect has a certain cigar-box elegance.

Charley comes out of his room to look and is immensely pleased. His face is wan, drained of everything but a thin wash of ecstasy. He wants Haselwood to go to Marin and climb Mount Tamalpais with him, but Haselwood says it is too late. Charley moves out of the room with the swiftness of a ferret.

Haselwood is relaxed, smoking. He looks at the blue alcove. "There is one more place I want to paint." He begins filling in a portion of the alcove with Ultra Gold.

Charley explodes into the room, looks at Haselwood on the ladder, and screams, "You can't bring the color of the earth to the sky of the alcove!" and is gone.

I don't know what is happening and am too tired to think about it. Pat and Lucille have made a pot of soup for supper. It's that time of day, and Moe and Doug have arrived with rumbling stomachs. A friend of Lucille's has dropped in with a toddler-sized baby under her arm, a withdrawn child with spun-silver hair sucking on a plastic bottle. Maggie is invited down from upstairs and we all crowd around the table, dipping into a huge pot of vegetable soup.

There is party in the air. Haselwood cuts to invite a young poet and his wife over. Charley and I pick up Justin's Persian rug to put on the floor of the Ultra Gold Room. The place is suddenly filled with people.

"Oh, oh," says Charley. "It's beginning. Before it's over I may have to move out and get a hotel room."

Joints are being passed like calling cards. There are so many people one joint won't even make it around the room. Daniel Moore, a young poet, has arrived with his wife, Gail, and with a strange thin spade in tow. Daniel is a horn-tootler and he has brought some of his instruments, long thin pipes from India, clay horns from Mexico, bamboo flutes. Charley has the radio blasting Ray Charles rock and roll. Daniel accompanies one of the numbers in a far-out kind of counterpoint. I am wigging out of my skull at the sounds. Haselwood is there ready for a musical trip to anywhere. He holds a black clay pipe from Oaxaca and he blows it shrilly in my ear. Blasts of sound are expanding rings of light in the vast darkness of my head.

Then the drag sets in. The horn-tootling goes on and on. The radio won't give up. Everyone is sitting in a dazed circle around the room.

The spade is restless. "Man, where are these people? Somewhere between the African beat and the Himalayas? Let's make it one or the other."

Somebody suggests dancing but nobody moves. Finally Moe gets on the floor, doing a kind of gentle twist, delicate and slight, with his big white body. The horn gets more frantic; Moe begins to move in awkward leapings and twirlings. His eyes are closed. His dance becomes a spasmodic twitching. It goes on and on. It is not beautiful to watch. Lucille heads for the kitchen. I'm close on her heels.

"The frankincense," she gasps. "Can't you smell it? I can't breath. It's everywhere!"

It is. Frankincense has permeated everything. There is no air that is not heavy with it.

Charley is right behind us. "What's happening to those people? What's going on? What's Moe dancing like that for? Has he flipped out?"

It's much warmer in the kitchen, where we sit now laughing

at the evening veering out of control.

"It never stops at Gough Street," says Charley. "Scenes just go on and on and on."

He's right. I step into the dining room for a moment, and there is innocent-looking curly-haired Maloney with an endpad spade laying out matchboxes of pot like cards in a game of solitaire. "Hey, man," the spade fuzzyvoices, "you got a cigarette?"

Back to the kitchen where Charley is getting more bugged by the moment. Suddenly the noise from the living room stops. It's a huge relief, a nasty scene may have been averted.

Charley and I head back to the living room. "Wait," I say, laughing hysterically. "What if he's still in there dancing even though the music has stopped?"

I'm thinking that is a silly impossible projection, but we are halted in the doorway by just that sight: Moe is still dancing, if dancing it can be called. His feet are moving in small jerky steps, his hands are clutching and clawing upward, his head is thrown back, his lips nuzzling and biting like an infant seeking a breast. All eyes are upon him, all except Pat's. She sits with one hand clasped over her mouth, her face averted. Quickly she gets up and leaves, seeking the sanctuary of her own room. Doug is on his back tossing the silver baby up and down. The sight of Moe stabs me like a knife and I bolt for the kitchen.

Lucille is there laughing and talking with the friend whose baby Doug is tossing. She hands me a recorder, "Here, maybe we can turn the tables with this."

We laugh together, and suddenly she is not a little brown girl scurrying away, but a warm, human being with kind and penetrating blue eyes. I'm lost in the charm of her. She is wearing a pale blue-and-white silky chiffon dress that leaves her throat and arms bare and falls in diaphanous folds about her body. Her skin is honey and her hair is glistening.

"I'm not used to scenes like this. I live in the country," she says. "So many people." She gasps and laughs, and for a moment her confusion makes everything all right.

In a moment Charley is back. His lips are drawn and his

face is chalk-white. "It's over," he says, "I told him to cut." Dead silence reigns in the house. One by one the people file through the kitchen with their coats in their hands. I grab Haselwood as he passes.

"What's happening?" I say. "What did Charley say?"

Haselwood is stiffnecked and withdrawn. "I'm going upstairs," he says. "You want to come up?" Daniel is with him, his instruments under his arm.

"Maybe later." I head for the front and meet Charley in the hall. His face is pale and purple around the edges.

"I told everybody to leave," he says. "But don't go yet. Stick around for awhile."

"Okay." I head on for the living room. Moe is still there and he is still dancing. Justin is alone with him. Back to the kitchen I go.

Now Charley and I smile at each other just a little.

"He's still dancing, Charley. What are we going to do? Just let him dance it out?"

"He stopped once, and Justin went over and told him that it's a world of joy and love, and he started in again."

A happy feeling like a roman-candle shower of sparks; I laugh at the wonder of Justin who with straightforward simplicity talks to madmen.

"We'd better find Doug," I say. "He knows him better than anyone else. Maybe he can get him calmed down." I dash upstairs.

Haselwood and Daniel are sitting quietly. I wonder if they're putting me down along with Charley.

"He's still dancing. What do you think we ought to do? Have you seen Doug?"

"Oh, he's still dancing?" Haselwood's eyes widen a little. I can see a faint trace of alarm. "Gee, I don't know. Maybe he'll just wear himself out."

"I was trying to get him calmed down with the music," says Daniel. "I would slow down the tempo and hope he would follow the music, but he just kept ignoring it and building up and going into another frenzy." The door opens and in walks Justin leading Moe by the arm. Justin's face is white and shining with love. Moe moves stiffly with Frankenstein steps. Justin puts him on a couch. He sits there muttering and clawing the air. No one knows what to do. I smile at him, trying to make some contact but he is not even within signaling distance.

I begin to talk, hoping we can dispel our fears and calm the atmosphere. "I really like those three illuminations I saw on the walls of your house," I tell Daniel. "They're very beautiful. I'd like to see some more of your work."

"Why, thank you," says Daniel and his face shows pleasure as he tells us about the illustrated book of poetry he has just finished.

But we can't talk any more because Moe has claimed our attention and riveted our concern to him. He strips his sweater from his body, holding it out, making breasts from it. He's cooing and laughing, his eyes are rolled back in his head. Now he sees ghosts in front of him. He makes loud incoherent noises that are almost words. The sounds are high pitched and grating, agonies ripping him apart. His breath is on the threshhold of screaming-animal cries. I catch a phrase or two as he calls upon God.

"For God's sake," he cries, and "God damn you." "Fuck, suck, fuck, suck," he moans, and then "What do you want to worry about things like that for?" He pleads with someone, he is imploring a throng of people who are walking around him. He foams at the mouth and I can take no more. I leave to try to find Doug. I meet him coming up the back stairs. "Help him," I beg Doug.

"He's in some kind of trance."

I find Charley downstairs in a world of woe, walking the walls.

"I've been crazy for three days," he says. "I've written a poem that may turn everything upside down. It's my love poem, my glory poem, and I talk directly to several people in it, trying to tell them where I am and what I have found out about things. One of the people I address is Moe, telling him that it is all all right. Now I don't know what I have done. Maybe I should just burn the poem. I don't know what's happening. It's all getting too fast," and on and on, torn and lamenting and confused and angry.

"Read me the poem, Charley," I say and he does, reading

over the sounds of strife coming from upstairs, over the interruption of Justin who comes in to listen and to tell us that they have taken Moe home. I listen as closely as I can to the best poem by far that Charley has ever written, a lament slashing out at the present-day American scene, hearing Charley bid us all to the find the glory that will overturn the world and extinguish the politics of nations. I tell him "It's great, Charley, it is great" and the poem, the pot, and Moe are all pushing and pulling inside my head and I want to run into the night, to burn the twisted energies of the world in fire streaming from my fingertips.

I cut for home with Justin, where I have dreams of strife and fire and shouting voices all night long. A fine first night christening for the room of Ultra Gold.

*
**

Goodbye. How can I leave these rooms where we have loved? That we beautified with life? No more music in the Blue Room, nor Justin-placed flowers on the round table pushing loveliness into the air, fulfilling space. The gold cloth comes down from above our bed of love, where more than once I lay awake in woe. The Blue Room gives up its books and paintings. There will be no more food on the turquoise table in the orange kitchen. How I have fallen from grace since I failed love!

We live in an earth world, not an ethereal world of spirit. And yet the spirit of Dan Rowan haunts these rooms, gestures and mimes to a Marlene Dietrich number. I'll swing no more to the Bossa Nova, it's antigua now. Mornings grey or sunny will not find me here, high or low, laughing in innocence or staring seared-faced into mirrors, struggling to make myself aware. We push forth into life, and measure out our days in rooms, rooms, rooms.

*
**

High on a ladder, transforming a dingy old storeroom into a place of light. Buttercup! and when that's gone, leftover orange from the orange kitchen for the woodwork. Up goes the cloth of

Above: "Do you have room for us, Charley?" Ginsberg & Cassady in front of 1403 Gough Strret, 1963. **Below:** Cassady behind the wheel, with Ann, Plymell and Ginsberg in the back seat. **Facing:** Neal and Ann, 1963

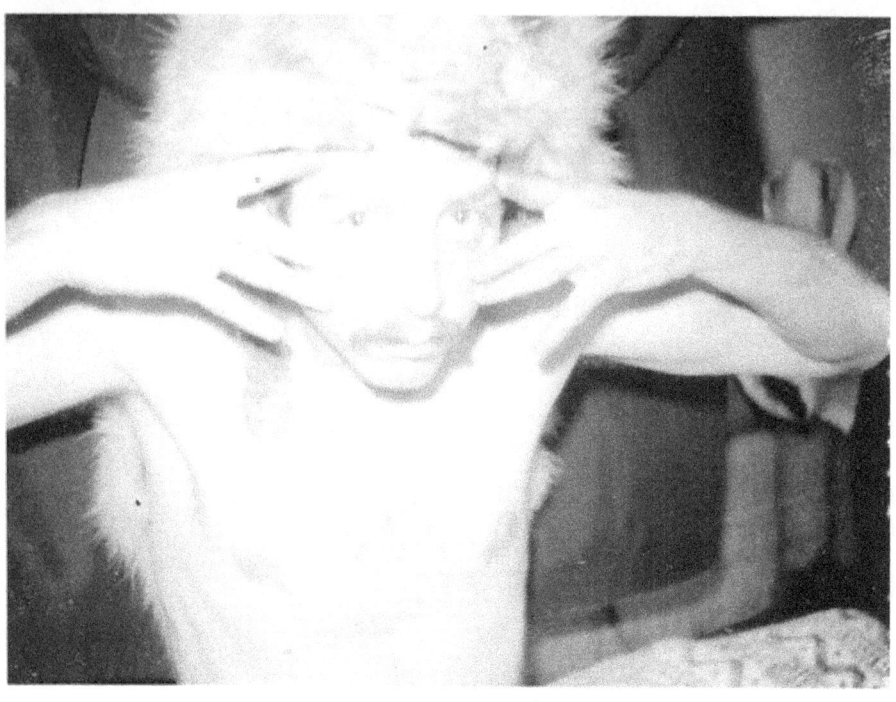

Above: Dave Haselwood in fox fur on Gough Street, 1963 (Photo © by Glenn Todd) Below: Charley Plymell, Patti & Janie, July 1963. (Photographer unknown)

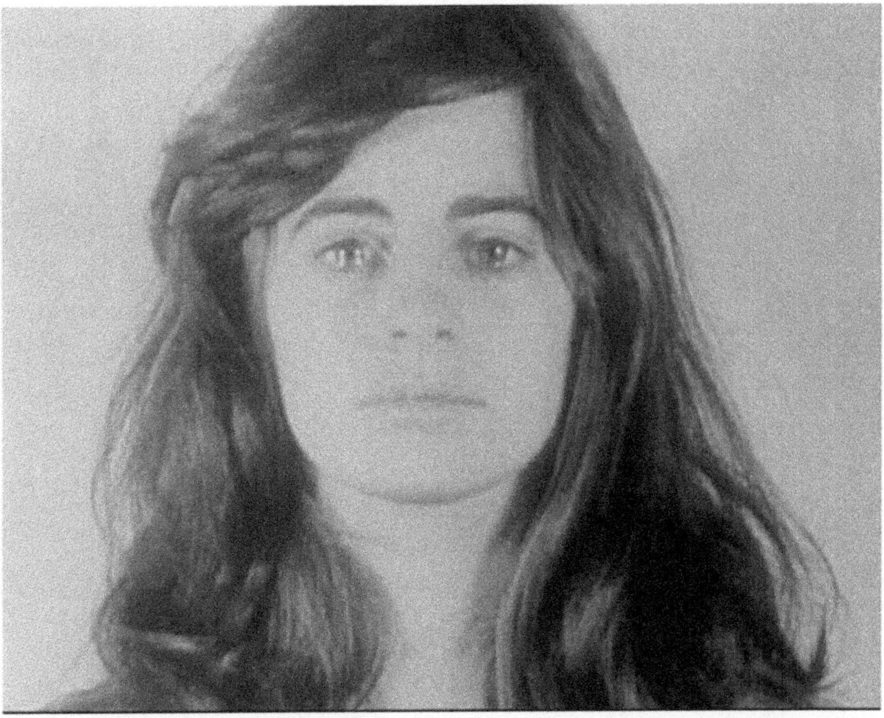

Above: Ann, Whalen, Plymell & Ferlinghetti in front of City Lights Books, 1963. **Below:** Ann Buchannan, Warhol's The Thirteen Most Beautiful Women Screen Test (Photo © by Gerard Malanga),

gold above the bed. In what sunbursts will Justin lie here! I can't stop now. I am possessed of an energy that shouts Clean! Make it bright! and for twelve hours I am on the ladder painting—white for the ceiling, gold for the chandelier, buttercup for the walls, orange for the woodwork, blue for the floor. Everyone is catching my act—Maggie has painted her kitchen floor, Haselwood is dressing his walls with paintings, drawings, shining the glass on his butterfly specimens, Charley is painting doors, throwing up wall hangings. Only Justin is somewhere in silent sadness; it's his last week on his skid-row job; he's leaving to pursue his Magnificat vision of Bach-bursting light and I can see the dark struggle toward self-love in his eyes and I long to cry Let me help, I can too love, but I can't stop now—I can only be ready to leap when the moment is gold.

Richard White comes by with his little boy and pulls me down off the ladder for coffee. He's growing a moustache and he's being very sincere and very definite. He is letting everyone know that he is quite serious about being a poet. He talks now the way he writes—in staccato bursts. He wants to start a press; he wants to be part of a new thing coming up; he wants to have a book for his beautiful wife and son. I admire his intentions. He compliments me; he tells me that I represent the imaginary audience for which he writes. He tells me that I am humble, and for awhile my starved ego is satiated. His son is beautiful, with reddish-gold hair and the still-bright face of babyhood. I look at Richard in a new light. I see that he is releasing bottled-up agony, that he is pushing forth in a new way. Maybe that is a genie pushing inside him and one day it will burst forth and astound us all with its magic. I climb back on the ladder in a glow from his youth and energy. He has strengthened my silent purpose: to reach for love when I am a bring-down or when I'm blue.

*
**

Charley Plymell and Haselwood are at war. Perhaps not in full scale attack but there are minor skirmishes along a line of demarcation. Haselwood brought the earth to the sky of the alcove when he refused to climb Mount Tamalpais with Charley to hear his poem. Charley hacked at roots of the tree of friendship when he put the ascent on a now-or-never basis. Charley wants Haselwood to help him publish his poem immediately; he demands help in the name of friendship. Haselwood wants all things in due course; he demands that his integrity not be sacrificed in the name of anything.

I dig and deplore the war. I dig the marshalling of forces, the gathering of wit, the fine lines of attack. I deplore the very real hurt and betrayal I see in both sets of eyes, the possibly permanent disruption of friendship that could occur. Being a pawn of some value to both sides, I am in a position to have first hand reports of the battle.

A still voice clad in Roman-toga dignity at the other end of a telephone: "Are you getting the Plymell treatment too?"

Christ eyes of betrayal, finding the Judas in every twelve, look up at me on the ladder: "Once I asked Haselwood if I wrote something that I thought was very good would he help me bring it out and he said yes."

And so on.

I feel trapped in no-man's-land and yet I do not wish to remain neutral if there is a real issue at stake. Coupling my imminent arrival in the double scene at Gough Street with my doubts about what I will find there, I moan, "Why does this have to happen now?" At first I think the best course would be to ignore the whole thing, but finally I decide to write it down in the book of friends and let it go at that.

*
**

Charley says: "You say you're moving in on Saturday? Do you mind if we have a party that night or would it be too soon? I've invited some people over already."

"Sure, whatever you feel like." Hmmmmm. What will that scene be?

Haselwood says: "I think we ought to give you and Justin a housewarming party the night you move in. I've invited the McClures, Phillip Whalen, and several others."

"Okay." My ears lift at the names. Is this an extension of

the war? Is Haselwood winning?

On Saturday as Justin and I are packing the last load, the telephone rings. It's Charley, coming on straight and solemn.

"You know that book of old masters Justin borrowed from me, do you have it over there or is it over here?"

"All the books are already over there in boxes but I wouldn't know where to tell you to look for it."

When we get there Charley is in the Gold Room. He has the book propped open on the mantel. It's open to reproductions of Pompeiian frescoes--angels and graceful nude women painted in browns and reds and golds. Charley is on the floor playing with Lucille's blonde friend and her silver-haired cherubic baby. He's laughing, out of his head again, and I assume he's smoked some grass.

At last it's all in, the swatches of cloth, the books, the records, the bed, the dishes--all the cumbersome equipment of living. Charley can't get the record player going, he's like Marian's inconsolable cats, he circles the table, touches the player, backs off, shakes his head. A look of utter bewilderment has come over him.

"I took a gram of mescaline a couple of hours ago," he confesses. "I can't stay here. Would you like to go for a walk?"

We strike the outside, pushing off down Gough Street toward Beat Faggot Park. I look at Charley, his face is drained and white with a slight purple cast at all the orifices. His misery is apparent and real; my pulse dips in sympathy at his pain.

"For God's sake, Glenn, get me to a hospital. I'm dying or flipping out. I've just been pulled through myself two or three times."

"Okay, Charley, but we'll have to walk. I can't magically wish us there. We can walk through the park and down Octavia."

"Anything. I've got to get to the hospital. I'm dying. I'm flipping out. What time does the hospital close? Will it still be open when we get there?"

***

I remember Charley, swinging. The time is spring-summer,

this year, 1963. The place, Wichita, Kansas, where the wheat has just been harvested and the trees are bursting greenery touching tips over the center of the streets. Charley stands in a combination teenage twist and gay bar done up in coral walls lined with gilded store-window manikins. He stands at the front of the dance floor before a jukebox that has a waterfall behind it. Light flows down the sides of the jukebox, so that he appears to be coming from a neon grotto. His hair is falling over his forehead in a mass of curls, he is wearing dark glasses, a blue-and-silver sport shirt, a metallic gold tie, tight black pants slung low on his hips, and black-and-white saddle oxfords. One hip is slung outward. Up go the hands in the air.

"TWIST!" shouts Charley.

Up his back runs a ripple like a snake moving, fast. His hips are inscribing a frenzied half-circle in the air. His head bounces and bobbles with jazz-drummer ecstasy. His arms flail, he's almost flying but his feet are planted in the floor, sucking up great electrical currents of earth vibrations.

"It's the vortex!" he shouts. "Can't you feel the forces! Pulling you in! It's twisting in twister land!"

Across the floor toward him dances his blonde college-girl goddess, and she's out of her gold pony-tailed head. She's all Charley could dream of exploding into, she's Miss Freeswinging Kansas, Caucasian aflame, descendant of hot-blooded fairy-tale princesses, she moves with classic American grace, she's poised and pure and fashion-hip, she has round arms of love, ready to grab, she won't be brought down, and above the rock and roll sweet cello strings play for all eternity in that golden head.

They're back at the table where a crowd of us are sitting. They're arm in arm, together again. I turn on to their beauty aglow with sex.

"This is where it all comes from!" shouts Charley. "Can't you feel the vibrations? Man, there is so much energy here that you just get near it and flooom! it's got you and swinging you some place else."

This is Charley's hometown, the land that produced him.

He's back to turn everyone on and get recharged. Everywhere he goes crowds of youth follow him, turning him on. Now the brown-limbed teenagers in cut-off jeans and bouffant hair have taken the floor. Their bodies are strong, sun-beautied and swimming-pool clean, they're eager-high on beer. They dance dances they all know, no one touching, boys with girls, girls with girls, boys with boys. All the steps are perfect and harmonious. They are all so beautiful that I know we cannot lose, mankind will take the stars and crush time with these dancing kids born of our bodies and spirit.

Here Charley is big, here with youth. He is vibrant with sex that knows no separation from love, and hope for and beware of the day its dancing force is turned on you, my friend. Crowds follow him, he is alive with scheme and dream. He will make it happen now. Are you ready? He will, like the morning glory but more aware, unfold himself in the sunburst of today.

Crowds follow him, turned on. He has a show of his collages at a weird place, the New Mission Cafe, in the skid row train station section of Wichita. Charley is aggrandizing, making bright the legend. Is it a game? How much is glory and how much is morning glory? (He quotes Cocteau: "All art is a card trick.") He has made the Wichita scene happen: bright-eyed campus beauties, long-haired students, careful college professors, waiting-in-limbo artists, shimmy-shake drag queens, long ago pill head buddies, strange inhabitants of the outposts of Beatsville—all come to soak up Charley, to be angered, to be inspired, to lift him up or put him down, but always to be stirred.

Wait! What is it that Charley sees? His eyes are wrestling with the world. The moment is now but now is not enough. What is it that Charley sees in the moment, each moment, that constantly extends itself beyond the time of now, so that he can never quite contain it? As I watch him push toward the Faustian moment of explosion, I would like to know why the moment must be now.

*
* *

We walk through Beat Fag Park. Charley is in the grip of

some fearful vise of what he thinks is incipient madness, a true moment of explosion. Little kids are playing with pieces of green broken glass.

I try to console him with stories. I tell him my Chipmunk peyote story about this park ("I give you that bouquet of tree," Chipmunk said solemnly, "to keep you high forever." And haven't I kept it, my lost somewhere little girl, last seen sleeping in culverts at Big Sur?) and other stories, chattering on and on sincerely, until I am sure he must see my game, that I am only playing for time. Block after block goes by, through the Tenderloin looking for a place to eat but it's another dope story—every place is closed or being repaired or the menu isn't right—somebody named Rose has put a poem in her cafe window warning everybody to be careful over Labor Day weekend. At last we hit upon a glass-and-chrome restaurant, and Charley confesses that he has survived again.

Then back to Gough Street. We remember the party and look at each other with what-will-happen-next eyes. Charley fixes the record player and we all turn on, but at nine o'clock no one has showed up except the regulars. I decide there will be no party, so in a state of exhaustion (painting, moving, Charley, and pot) I take to my bed, my new bewildering abode, and zonk! I'm out.

*
**

I awaken to sounds of people at the front door, and then standing by my bed, immediately, is Joanna McClure and her daughter, Jane. The dress Joanna is wearing is a subdued red, like the blush of my favorite rose.

She smiles at me, looking at me, and pulls an answering smile from my creaking being. "We came to have a welcoming party for you and Justin, and here I find you in bed."

""Hello, Glenn," says Jane. "I came to the party to see where you live but I have to go to bed."

They move on upstairs to put Jane to bed with Maia.

I heave my chest in a quick prayer to a god somewhere to awaken my brain but I receive no answer. I move toward the sounds of laughter in the Gold Room. People are everywhere—but suddenly I wish for even more so that I can lose myself among them. Big names have arrived: Allen Ginsberg, a burning saintly poet, now famous, home from the Far East bringing with him the orient pearl of wisdom (his hair and beard obscure everything but his blazing eyes; I page in vain through remembered photographs to see his face); and a publisher-poet, Ferlinghetti, a large man burning with the coals of indignation, eyes searching a wilderness plain.

People have filled the Gold Room. I'm interested in these people but I wish only to watch, to have no demands made upon me. I want to see them by firelight. I build a fire, but just a small one, afraid that the heat will drive everyone away. At last I am a little more collected. Richard White's beautiful wife, Cheryl, a purely American combination of little girl and glamor, comes toward me. She wears a crystal pendant across her forehead. Her talk soothes me. Richard himself is dressed like a Mississippi gambler--vest, tie, and slender cigar.

"Oh, so you're taking a chance on being a gambler," I say, liking his dash. "If you're dealing, deal me in." Later he slips me a card. The Jack of Spades. I complain that it is not the Ace of Hearts.

Pot is flowing like wine, and at last the wine is beginning to flow, someone having sent out for some. I take a toke every time the pipe passes but I cannot bring myself to drink. I am an inconsolable cat; I wander from room to room watching. Michael McClure is in the kitchen doing the buddy bit with two beefy guys, one of whom is huge and awkward. The big one crushes a beer can and kicks it across the kitchen. McClure is cool, I'm watching, hoping that somehow he is in charge.

"Nothing like being matter of fact," McClure says to Joanna. I wonder of what the comment is apropos. I think he means I should take charge, kick the guy out of this pad I moved into a few hours ago, but I can't take charge of anything.

I see Phillip Whalen's handsome face across the Gold Room. He is dancing, all night long he is dancing. Controlled grace and *joie de vivre*. I look at his face. His grace is dearly bought and paid for with the high coinage of self-made serenity.

He has beatified himself. I can feel him asking me to let him help me relax. No matter what the music--Bach, Bossa Nova, Ray Charles—he dances his stately pleasurable dance. His is a dear example that demands no disciple.

Moe is off again. The music is too much, being unnoticed by so many people is too much. He's down on his knees in the middle of the room, going under. Charley grabs him by the arm, "Come on, Moe, let's take a walk," and he leads him into the hall, but Charley doesn't really want to leave the party, the moment is now, so I take Moe to my room. He's breathing heavily, his eyes are rolled back in his head. I stand before him, I brush his long fallen hair back from his forehead. I want to pat his cheek. I pat his cheek. He looks at me, breathing heavily. I see in his eyes my limitations as a comforter, and leave him be. He returns to the Gold Room and begins again, but Ginsberg has fixed him with his eyes and leads him away.

Cheryl and I are back to back. We want to dance, really dance, but we can't. I can feel the dance in her body, trying to make me to let go. We bounce our asses together and it is fun. Richard ties us together with a sash. Soon I cannot bear it. I am tied to Cheryl, and backwards. My fingers work nervously at the knot until it is undone. Someone asks for pot and I dance in the middle of the room while rolling a joint. I catch a glimpse of Moe as he springs at me from the couch, like a football player. I am thrown to the floor, the pot flung wildly (half a lid), someone's wine poured upon me like a libation. I'm down. I'll swing no more this night. I leave the room.

What is there in a man, when he sees someone swinging, what is there in him that desires to cut the swinger down, to bring him down to his level, to erase ecstasy from his face and replace it with his own misery? Why can we not let the force of others flow through us, not against us, possess us even? Here wars are born.

I pass the omnipresent Phil Whalen. The eighteenth-century courtier moves back through time toward Rabelaisian gusto. "Drinks only water," he comments instructively to my empty hand.

McClure is at the front door with the big guy, who is going

down the stairs. "And a package of fig newtons. Can you remember that?" says McClure, wearing a fierce enigmatic smile.

The big guy pauses for a moment, crushing beer cans in his mind. "Hey, man, you putting me on?" I'm impressed by McClure's tightrope skill.

How to flush the failing bird of fatigue? These people, are they not my guests? Baby-food jars from Maggie's kitchen for the wine.

Charley and Phil Whalen are dancing together. Each has a white muff on one hand. To the music of Mozart they come toward each other, like courtiers, like swordsmen, like timid lovers reaching out. They touch hands, unite, and break away.

Through these rooms of night the face of Justin in pale firelight shies toward shadow, the fear of proffered love refused dwindling him toward extinction. Maggie eases her way in the room, like a wary child, sees me, extends herself with words but somehow wrongly, and I strike back at her. Failure, again! Maggie, oh Maggie, don't hit me where I'm weak, I'm only a man. Next time, I hope I'll be more adroit. Phil Whalen has watched. He consoles my failure with a smile from across the room.

I can ignore Justin no longer. I hover around him as inconspicuously as I can. I murmur nothings sweet as I can muster into his ear. He can't hear me, "What," he says, "what did you say?" trying to listen. ("Speak louder, for I am deaf," said Beethoven.) I push my way to his side, to let him calm my fear. We lean toward each other.

"You look like two lost children," the clear voice of McClure reaches me. For a moment I see him purely.

"What?" whispers Justin in my ear. "What did he say?"

I bend toward Justin in warm, embarrassed love.

As the McClures leave, I apologize for my negligence. Joanna's voice comes to me like bread from forgotten waters, spontaneous with forgiveness. "I'm not going to let you get away with that, Glenn, come around at the last moment playing the host, and try to smooth things over."

Silly power games tumble like children's blocks with my

only pleasurable laugh of the evening.

And Haselwood, why he's here and there, calling it a wonderful party, easily appearing and disappearing.

But why delay the truth. I did not make it—that whirling world of community. Only the dance with Cheryl, only the rose-blush space of Joanna kept me from going under. At some bewildered point I tumble to bed to let myself be drawn through darkness by the chariot of party horses who won't stop till dawn.

Oh gentle reader, who do you think came to my bed with sweet-father goodnight kisses, placing roses on my cheek with thorny beard scratches? Who? Did you guess it would be—my branch of Haselwood?

I'm the first awake. Is this life on Gough Street? Is this the way it will be? I must get out. Justin is right behind me, listening while I flail humanity on its old rugged cross. I'll move, I'll go, I can't transform Gough Street, it's too much, I'll find a cozy quiet place, do you want to come with me, Justin? You think Gough Street has something to offer you, do you? What? Paranoia! Filth! Power struggles! Laziness! Boredom! The endless! downhill! trek! toward! endpadism! I dig it not. My energies are limited, I'm only human etc. etc.

Justin buys me breakfast as a consolation prize.

We meet Charley on the front steps. I look for answers. He gives me one I need: an assurance that last night was only a party and not an ongoing scene. He cools the big boy in my head bending beer cans and kicking them through the kitchen walls.

I'm off—wash scrub fix putter. "What are you so upset about? Why are you working yourself to death? It'll be here tomorrow." And tomorrow and tomorrow. I will, said the little red hen. While I am high on my ladder screwing in a light bulb, an electric thought strikes me: Where was Marian last night? Who did not invite her? I should have seen her across the room, slicing the smoky air with her gliding hands. She would have sought me out, moved toward me through all the people, like a little girl stepping carefully among flowers in a garden.

※

The palm reader, a strange sideways boy-painter named Joseph, looks at my hand. He tells me, "You are morbid. Your life has been completely fucked up till now, then it's like you explode and wow! you want power. At one point in your life you are obsessed with money." I give him not an inch to go on. I make him tell him me everything with no feedback. I am shaken. Frightened. Power you want. Obsession with money.

Charley confirms his fortune with nods and smiles of agonized sadness. Justin listens carefully and sincerely explains his life to Joseph. I miss Haselwood's fortune, I'm out of the room. McClure leaves as the palmreading begins.

※

I am practicing looking at Pat.

"It is a terrible thing to feel isolated," says Pat.

I look at her. We are seated at the round mahogany table. Her face is large and blank, like a flower, and it sways and droops on the stem of her slender neck. I hold her before my eyes like a Nolde watercolor. I cannot bear it and drop my eyes.

Contact! Justin has thrown himself at me, and I have caught him as best I can. He cushions my rigidity. I pull him from his dark retreat. We must hold our relationship to light. We must examine it, turn it in our hands. We must dismantle it, reconstruct it at a moment's notice. We push each other onward to love.

Up to Maggie's kitchen to borrow garlic powder.

"What's the matter, Maggie? You look like you have been crying."

"No, I haven't been crying. Maia's been crying. I've been peeling an onion."

But she had been crying. Maggie, where are you? In a fat girl's dream? I dig those round thighs of yours. You're a Reubens come to life. You'll have to grow more than flesh to keep me away.

※

In the old ghost room Charley is staring out the window, down into the old trashy driveway. He looks around when I walk in, then looks away. His handsome face is in mourning. The brown curls fall over his furrowed brow.

"I love it when you get sad," I say. "You're beautiful when you're sad."

He tries to smile at my banter. He throws something in the trash basket and walks away.

I fish out the crumpled paper and smooth it, then read it. It's a poem:

> I don't know why
> The sky
> Fell on my patchwork quilt that day
> Crushing my strawberries
> Leaving me in a baby's dream
> Beyond repair.

I fold the paper and carefully put it away with my things.

※

I cook. I like feeding people. I like to be liked for what I do more than for what I am. I waver at each instant of action, then leap. Sometimes I fall. I fix the dishes of home. Banana pudding. Swiss steak. Pies.

For banana pudding you thicken a mixture of flour, sugar,

and egg yolks, flavored with vanilla; pour over layers of bananas and vanilla wafers; top with beaten egg whites; brown meringue topping in oven.

While I am thickening the sauce, pretty curly-haired Maloney is sitting at the kitchen table, eating my seedless grapes by the handful, telling me how easy life is in San Francisco. Chomp! I am barely there, the sauce is taking too long. Suddenly Moe appears in the doorway.

"Man, how did you get in here?" I'm startled and shocked.

"I came through a window." He laughs nervously, almost coquettishly.

"There's a door you can knock on," I say fiercely.

"I, I, I was afraid you would think I was a ghost."

"I'll take that chance."

So I cook. I hope someone will help me. Sometimes I yell at Justin. An indulgent attitude is all I ask from Charley. Pat must be coaxed like a vine. What do they think? Do they think I do this out of a faggot love of kitchen?

Blasted out of our heads. We are happy at Gough Street. I feel like the big spray of lilacs from the tree next door. Or the bowl of orange Jello filled with peaches in the refrigerator.

Charley dances from room to room. He has an idea for starting a magazine. That way he can publish his glory revolution poem, as well as giving voice to others. He feels the forces rising, pushing down the evil of government. He sees the Big Sur golden rovers gathering strength to burst upon the world. He's a sexual messiah, a pied-piper for teenagers. He convinces me: I see them dancing in savage joy, with bracelets of morning glories. This is the moment, now. The idea for a magazine has been whirling in his head for a couple of years. Let it come to light.

MICHAEL MCCLURE is here. The name is HUGE and

BURNING, like his POETRY! He enters a room with flourish, he enters a room like a hound or a jaguar, sniffing all corners, exploring all avenues of escape before sitting down. Agonized, exhausted, radiating romance and energy, he enters a room as if it were a stage. He steps down into the audience, does a graceful dance among us. He enters a room sullenly, his eyes puffy and swollen, turned inward, burning holes in his heart. He enters a room like a questing spirit: he sees us, he demands to see us.

He's turned me on. He's allowed me to see him. He's started a great force moving in my head, like a wind or a rock slide. I cannot escape it. I am interested in his ideals.

He is by profession a poet and married to Joanna, boy slender, girl round. He has a daughter, Jane, seven years old. He has no son. They live in white rooms. On the wall the head of a fierce bird demands acknowledgement. A hymn he has written to youth is pinned to the fireplace mantel. Mike and Joanna sleep together on a wide bed on the floor. Sometimes I think of them locked in the act of love, on the pale velvet coverlet, in the feral air, in the den of gods.

He has no pity. He's poised to the point that he annihilates other-ness. Mike, Justin, and I sit in the white rooms, zooming through space on pot. Mike is playing the piano, a spontaneous composition entitled "The Life and Death of Mandrake the Magician." It is very tricky. Justin is delighted and he plays a composition called "Goodbye to Orphan Annie." I'm relieved to see Annie's wide round eyes finally close. It is my turn. I will play "Alley Oop in the Time Machine."

At the piano I freeze. I feel compelled to take seriously the absurd, and I wish I could evaporate. I'm a cold stone plummeting. My mouth pulls inward with anal retentiveness. I blank my head and attack the keyboard. All memory of what follows (except the crash of bravado) leaves me forever.

I'm in an armchair, head in hand. I hate these oneupmanship games. Paralyzed, I watch Justin and Mike watching T.V., relaxed. Why can't I just blot us all out?

Joanna comes in from ironing and comes to the point. "Glenn, you look sick. You must have gotten hold of some green pot. Your face is green. I've seen it happen before."

Hideous, paranoid forces unite in my brain and enthrone Jealousy, green-gilled potking. I feel my blood drain away all blue, leaving me yellow with fear. I take a deep breath. I look at my hands and summon love. ARTERIAL RETREATS ARE NOT IN ORDER! I declare the star system null and void. Goodbye, Jesus, goodbye, Valentino.

In the orange kitchen on the turquoise table dripping skeletons of crab are piled like losers on a battlefield. Mike and Joanna arrive. Mike is hungry. I offer him crab.

"Is it good crab?" he asks suspiciously.

"Tasted good to me. They're fresh. A friend who trapped them brought them to us. I enjoyed them."

"I'll be able to tell you." Of course he will. "I'm a connoisseur of crab." He is a connoisseur of everything. He winks at me conspiratorially (or is that a nervous tic?). His mouth is full. "Ummm. It's good crab. Excellent crab." I believe him, now I can enjoy the crab.

Despite my ambivalent feelings, Mike has turned me on. His men are angels, his women are goddesses! He walks down the street holding his daughter's hand. They stride into clear air, they slide with grace around corners. Almost unnoticed by me, he has handed me a message, a chance for freedom: the key of self-kindness fits the lock of anxiety. He leaves quickly. His eyes are preternaturally alert. He's gone in a burst of energy.

Wait! He has left a black spot dancing before my eyes. What is it? is it a hawk? is it a spaceship? is it a tornado? is it a snake? is it an angel? is it a final point of implosion? Naw, it's Superpoet.

*
**

Zoom! Off like a spaceship we blast. We're carrying the old house on Gough Street right up to the stars.

Charley stops me in the ghost room, Marian's old room when she lived here. "Hey, man." He looks at me. His eyes have the veiled look of animals, the heavy gaze of the bull as it swings its head around. His sexy look.

"No," he says, changing his mind about something. "I shouldn't talk to you about business when we're high."

"Go ahead, Charley. It's all right."

"Well, you know this magazine I am going to bring out? I'm going to need a business manager to help me. In fact, I'll need lots of help."

A cold hand snatches my heart away; he knows about the money I have saved at my drudge job. "Okay, Charley, I'll give you any kind of help you want but money. I can't afford to put any money into anything. But anything other than that. I'll be glad to help anyway I can. Okay?"

It's okay. He keeps talking. Soon it becomes obvious that he wants money. Five hundred from me and five hundred from Justin. To be paid back, of course. I am infuriated with myself and with him. How dare he ask me for the money I have saved so I could write in freedom! How dare I think of refusing him!

"I'll have to think about it. I'll let you know tomorrow. As for Justin, you'll have to ask him."

How terribly swift a rising balloon can be popped! I tell Justin to go see Charley. As I pace the hall I see them in the kitchen talking earnestly together.

I think of Charley's reaction when I asked him if we could move in. "Yes," he said immediately. A quick decision based on, I thought, love. When Charley walks down the hall, I stop him. "Okay, when do you want the money?"

"The sooner the better. Tomorrow, if possible. Justin's said okay, too."

Turmoil, anger boiling up from muddied depths. How dare he ask, how dare I refuse? Most of the night in my bed, the demon of self-preservation wrestles with the demon of altruism. Sometimes the wrestlers roll out of my head across the white sleeping form of Justin. What muscular arms each has! At some point I fall asleep and awake with the two demons merged into the angel of self-respect, and it carries a flaming sword of indignation. The angel swings the sword.

"I'm getting out of here," I shout at a sleepy-eyed Justin.

"Gough Street is too fucking much! Strangers at the food, friends at my money. Me working my ass off and everybody putting me down for it." I hear Lucille and her friends scurrying for cover out of doors.

Justin looks at me pale and ethereal from across the table. "If you don't want to give Charley money, then don't. But I think it is a matter of having enough faith in him."

"Faith in Charley, my ass. Charley works. Let him save his money if he wants a goddamn magazine. Why should he come to me if he wants money? I'm not working, he is. But he'll soon have me working. He wants to bring out that goddamn thing out once a month! Do you know how much work is there? I'll do all the work and spend all the money and he'll get all the glory. Faith in Charley! If he had any fucking faith in himself, he would have had that magazine years ago when he first thought of it." Etc., etc. The swinging sword is wearing away under the shielded eyes of Justin.

I find a note from Charley asking Justin or me to meet him at City Lights Bookstore on his lunch hour.

"You go. I won't. I'm getting out of this fucking place."

But somehow I'm the one that goes. I have a simple solution. I'll become a partner. I'll put in some money and he can put in some money.

On the way to meet Charley, I meet Haselwood and Moe at the bus stop. The bus is coming. "Quick, Haselwood, give me a capsule opinion on a magazine by Charley."

"I think he should do it."

"What about money? He wants some from me."

"Don't put in much. Don't put in any if you don't want to."

I feel a surge of power and I'm off to meet Charley. I'm a magazine publisher. Everything unites with mechanized precision in my head. People! I can do anything with them. Political me! moving with sureness among the pangs of artists. The Christ-total of my years falls in the dust at my feet. I could weep for joy with all the hard work ahead.

Whoa, I have plunged past my stop. I'm almost to Market. I cut back and head for Grant Avenue, doing the blocks at a steady clip. I look into the eyes of the Montgomery Street people. Hello, furs, hello jewels. Don't get in my way today.

At City Lights Charley looks up from among the magazines. He's withdrawn and down, but that doesn't stop me. I am asking a thousand questions about what he wants. Format. Authors. Costs. The works.

"This is the way I see it, Charley," and I tell him. "Quality plus sensationalism. But just once thing. Partners. Fifty-fifty all the way. Equal editorial voice."

Charley glances up at the word partners.

"I can get anything from anybody you want, just tell me who," I continue.

"I prefer to keep it free from politics as possible."

"So do I, Charley, free as possible." I'm out to win. I know I can make it work. I carry the salve in my hip pocket to anoint the wounds of countless sides. What is sweeter than the kiss placed on the cheek of another that singles him out from all the rest? Let Charley have the glory, I'll make it run. I can't stop now. I'm off. Goodbye, Charley.

And hello, Glenn. You don't want to bind yourself to some little magazine. The money you saved is for freedom, not something to chain you in some dingy Fillmore backroom to a machine you have never seen before. Of course you won't do that. Just let Charley have your money and mark it down in the book of friends if it isn't returned. What to do? What to do? Find Haselwood.

I grab Haselwood at his press and we go out for coffee. We land in a corner booth, alert with the idea of Charley's mag, plunging like raptors, pecking like two corbies. Screech, hop, jerk, caws of laughter, flutters of alarm. We devour with the tiny beaks of logic. We go over the possibilities and impossibilities of success. At last a calm comes over me, I feel battered, but the birds have flown and I'm still alive. Haselwood has once again made me see that I alone must decide what I alone am doing.

I can't resist voicing a final doubt. "What bothers me, is just how much is glory and how much is morning glory. And I don't mean just Charley, I mean me, I mean all of us."

"That morning glory business," says Haselwood. "You know, I think I started all that. Remember when we were listening to Marlene Dietrich and I said she sounded like the voice of a black morning glory. That was way before people started taking those morning glory seeds. Then Charley made something of it. Besides, hoe-ney, remember the morning glory lasts one day only. And it's only beautiful at dawn. The rest of the time it's folded up." A final parting shot in the war?

∗
∗∗

I'm preparing dinner. How am I going to tell Charley he can't have my money? I am afraid Charley's paranoid wrath will be focused on me. If the magazine is aborted, who will be responsible? I see the knife of my decision scraping the pregnant womb of his imagination. No, no, I won't do that. Oh, oh, will Charley understand?

"Just tell him," says Justin. "Charley doesn't expect you to do anything you don't want to do?"

"I know he doesn't, but it is a matter of his being able to recognize that I'm not just some figure of his imagination and that if he does this I will do that. I'm not an extension of anyone, I'm a free agent. If Charley doesn't understand, he will see me only as someone who didn't obey the laws of friendship. Therefore I'm to be cut down because I'm a force moving against him, possibly to do him in. I'm not saying this will happen, I'm saying it's a possibility. I don't want to lose Charley's friendship and I'm afraid it hangs on this."

The icy calm of decision settles over me. I will steer my ship straight toward those uncharted, iceberg seas. I dread Charley's arrival but when he comes in he is relaxed and down. He doesn't talk about the magazine and it's obvious he's glad to have friends around him. I postpone the moment. Let him eat a good supper first. He may need the nourishment. I feel him picking up on my anguish.

"There are some really strange forces out today." He shakes

his head with sad knowledge.

A quiet moment. Shall I speak? Suddenly there is a knock at the door. Charley comes back smiling, pulling someone into the kitchen—it's mad Roxie! one of Charley's oldest friends—back from Germany and he's looking brown and healthy, full of new wild stories and thousands of new perceptions, interested and ready to take Charley for a skydive. I see a moment of escape that depends on instantaneous action.

I leap for a fifth of vodka, which I have providently stashed in the cupboard in case of emergencies. (All day long it's been sending out its siren music to me.) I wave the bottle in the air, like a weapon or a prize, and I hear my own voice shouting, "I'm glad to see you back, Roxie, I want to hear all your stories, but you'll have to excuse me tonight, and, Charley, I can't make that magazine scene with you!"

Charley pushes his chair back, his hand raised to pacify, I hear him say, "Wait a minute, man, don't do anything rash!", a look of concern and comprehension in his eyes that makes the veil of otherness fall away instantly.

But it's too late. I'm off.

I run down Gough Street clutching my vodka, I'm swifter than the wind, they can't catch me. At Geary I turn toward Fillmore, flashing past sunset rubble and weeds and parked cars gleaming and useless and stationary. Gradually I become aware of something else moving out there, the traffic of slow cars and dim figures. I think of radar police eyes scanning my fleeing figure. I pull up, glance back over my shoulder, and look for a paper sack to cover my vodka. There it is in the gutter, ripped and weathered.

Nowhere to go. I'll go back to Delmar Street, I'll sit in the Blue Room and get drunk, I'll pass out in the orange kitchen. Ghosts will dance round my unconscious figure. Or I'll go to Buena Vista park. The cruising queens will have gone home. I'll crawl in a cave of dark leaves and nuzzle my bottle. When I come home everyone will be in bed. No one will question a man too drunk to answer. I'll go to Mike and Joanna's, they'll take me in, especially if I am already so drunk the fine lines of etiquette are blurred.

Fillmore slides past swiftly, silently. What clouds, what

black clouds hang on Fillmore Street this day, my heart, my sometime love. Up Haight Street and a stop for a bottle of tonic water for a chaser. An Oriental man counts my change back to me with detachment. I lean over the pool of his calmness, inexplicably attracted, but I move on quickly.

A Volkswagen passes. I see the scarfed necks of Mike and Joanna go by. They are talking and don't see me wave. At Buena Vista I climb a cement stairway that leads to black greenness, but up ahead I see a police car, fag-searching spotlight moving among the trees. Not that way. I settle on the lower slopes by the swings. The park is dark and the sky is lavender veering swiftly toward purple. A wind rises and the fog moves in, violet-charcoal, blotting out the sky. I sit in a swing, rocking aimlessly. Pieces are falling into place and yet the puzzle is not solved. I am lifted above the city into the sky but I can't escape. I see my solitary figure looking at the world. I listen for its thoughts: I hear it trying to describe exactly the colors of the night.

I leave the swing and huddle on a park bench, clutching my vodka tightly between my thighs. It's not so bad here. I take a big gulp and hold my breath. Ugh, but I can drink it. I wonder what everything will be like when I'm drunk. Foolish man. Go somewhere and fold your arms and wait. I lift the bottle again. I hold my breath for a long time. I light a cigarette and look out over the city. It's still out there. That furnace glow of sky is caused by it. The wind makes a low hollow sound as it blows over the mouth of the vodka. A touch too much. I have to laugh. But I'm cold. I take a few more drinks until I feel the bottle is lighter in my hands. Why ain't I drunk? It's not bad here. The wind whistles over my vodka bottle again. I don't laugh a second time. It's cold here, my knees are aching and where can I go?

Delmar Street, our old empty apartment. At least it's out of the wind. But it's lonely there. Ghosts are no company, especially if you don't even believe in them. Take a chance, maybe that wasn't Mike and Joanna you saw. I duck into a laundromat and dial their number. Joanna's voice focuses its attention on the receiver.

"Hello," it says clearly.

"Hello," I say slowly, playing for time. "This is Glenn. How are you?"

"Well, all right. How're you?"

"I was wondering if you are receiving tonight. I need to escape from Gough Street."

"Uh, Mike is over at your place, and I was just getting ready for bed. Where are you?"

"On Haight. Just a little way away."

"Okay, come on over."

"Ten minutes."

Mike isn't there. I bite my lip in consternation. But wasn't it Joanna I wanted to see, all along?

I shout up the stairway and Joanna's voice comes back. "It didn't even take you ten minutes."

I wave my bottle and she brings in ice cubes. A fire is going in the grate, small flames curling around a log. She is wearing high heels and wheat jeans that hug her hips. Across her breasts is a silk blouse of a field of pale yellow flowers.

First thing I ask: "How much money does someone have the right to ask for in the name of friendship?"

"Not one penny," she says authoritatively.

She laughs and asks questions, and I can't help laughing as I answer. I tell her about my troubles with Charley. It comes out in laughter and diminishing nervousness. Now I glide over the memory of the whole day, with only an occasional wingflutter of anxiety. I feel the bruised edges of my being dissolving. I'm in this room, now, the firelight is soft, this is a night on earth, a warm woman is across the room from me, laughing.

Wait. She's not laughing. Her hand rests lightly under one breast. She leans against a white wall, her head drooping slightly, her eyes gazing to one side and focused somewhere beyond this room. I see that she is hurting. That she is tired. That she has answered the call of friendship. Now she has remembered some pain of her own.

"What's the matter?"

"I've had this pain in my side for some weeks now. I'm worried as to whether it is something organically wrong or whether it is psychosomatic, not that it makes any difference. I just want to know what it is."

We gravely discuss the pains of bodies, but I can hardly keep track of what we are saying. Borne on the rising tide of vodka, another force is tossing upon the waves in a locked chest, pulled from this day's roiling depths to the shore of now.

The chest is at my feet. I marvel at its strong construction, its seamless execution. I look at Joanna across the room, I see her concern and self-concern, I see her hand at the vague pain in her side. I think of her kindness that came like a flower opening. I hear the hideous midair chirpings of the shoreline swallows of incapability darting through the air. I spring the lock.

"I want you to know, in case it can ever be of consolation to you, that I love you."

She gazes at the jewel from my chest. I have caught the lady's eye, and she's watching. I am not through. The jewel has many facets. Has my lady seen all? Waves of drunkenness sweep over me. The chest is overturned. I'm a little boy. Look, you'll like this one!

"Not that I would love you only sitting across the room. I tell you this only because you might need to know. Since the night I met you years ago and we tried to start a fire in your fireplace and couldn't get it going, was that an omen? and on and on—you in a blue dress and laughter and a black skirt and black hose and blue eyes and wisps of your hair falling," and now I don't know if I'm saying words or just thinking them "your body slender and yet so round your small hands me on a high rock at the beach your husband watching you in my Mexican sweater now magical fleece you sidestep a wave spindrift across your eyes your husband large almost blocking my view with the hawk's beauty of his protective eyes you reaching to hit a tennis ball you quiet on grass or beside Guatemala lakes and streams and riding your girlhood horse your life a movie being filmed somewhere of everything you do I see you warm woman stepping forward not waiting I have a thousand snapshots that I can call upon at will—"

"You keep a photograph album?" Her laughter is contagious.

What have I done? Look at this beach. Is it strewn with wreckage or treasure? Joanna moves across the room to stir up the fire.

"How do you reconcile your two loves?

"My two loves?"

"Yes. You love Justin, don't you?"

Bong goes the reveille gong. My two loves. I had not remembered there were two. "Yes, I love him. I love him because — because I'm—I love him the way I love Jane."

When I say it I feel a lie tingle. Once that was true perhaps, but no longer. Justin glows in my head beyond protection.

I give myself over to the waves of drunkenness, I cavort, I wallow, I blow sprays into the air. "I hear Mike coming," she says. Sure enough, the whirr of a Volkswagen cutting through the water.

I hold up the last jewel, a tawdry necklace dripping seawater. "Don't tell Mike what I said, because I—because he—"

"I wasn't even thinking about that," Joanna says gaily and disappears down the hall. I sit very still. I hear Mike's voice on the stairway, very clear, very strong.

"Glenn came here?"

I summon all my powers of concentration but I can't understand what he is expressing. Is it truly only surprise?

*
**

Waiting for sleep in my bed on Gough Street, I lie awake far into the night. Human behavior in endless plot variations flashes through my head. Where am I? What am I doing? Who are they out there? What is this thing called friendship? How do we fit into it?

I call my name into the dark. Glenn. Glenn. I, Glenn, the little red hen. I tremble with recognition. I see myself doing, being. I stir the universe to action. I cannot stop it. I see Justin. He is working on a mural at the end of the hall. He's cooking supper. He's taking care of Maia while Maggie paints the floor. He, Justin, the little red hen. I stare at the mystery of otherness. I am filled with the illusion of individuality. What is a mirror? I see my eyes red-rimmed with tears in the face of Marian. I see my forehead wrinkle with Maggie's doubt. I see my face light up when Justin loves. My lips smile when Charley laughs. I see in my glass Jane McClure's innocence shake its blonde head. I see Haselwood's courage peer out at me. I see the hawk-thrust of McClure's determined wit. I see Moe's eyes roll upward flipping out.

Long into the night I lie very still, resting. People move through my head. I give them action but they are not my puppets. LET US BELIEVE IN THE FOLLY OF WIRES WHICH JERK US! They stand in landscapes of primal awe. They stride through space naked or covered with brightness, bathed in white light or held in shadow. I name them friends. Why do they move through my head till dawn? I give them action but they have taken over. When, oh when, will I forget who they are, who I am?

I lift my hand toward the black reaches of space. I strive for the creation of a god that can encompass nothingness. I do not seek consolation. I am beyond pity. I am awake, at rest. GOD SITS IN THE UNUSED PORTION OF MY BRAIN! I fall backward in time, through blood and bone, through carapace and claw, through frond and fin and cilia. I fall to quirk in slime to rock to fire to explosion to struggling forward to remembering who I am where did I come from what is that out there walking inside my brain. I am the mind of a god awakening.

When did I fall asleep?

POSTSCRIPT 1997

Her ende teh litel boc of freonden in medias res. The friends were long-lived. Only one, to the knowledge of the chronicler, died in the thirty-four years that passed between the time he pushed away from the journal and the time he peered into the computer to make fair copy. Some of the friends stayed in San

Francisco; one left for the countryside; many moved half a nation away; still another put the continent between him and California; others were lost in time. Glenn continued to live in Gough Street for many years.

POSTSCRIPT 2009

Hold on a minute, I have to say something. I have to say "synchronicity", defined by the American Heritage Dictionary as "coincidence of events that seem to be meaningfully related; simultaneity". I stumbled across RealityStudio, had never seen it before, and don't remember how I got here, but was immediately snagged by a small reproduction of a magazine cover I remember well and once possessed, Charley Plymell's NOW. So I began to read the article by Jed Birmingham on collecting William Burroughs. He wrote of the Olympia edition of "Naked Lunch", the very one I cut my Burroughs teeth on in 1960. That particular copy belonged to Dave Haselwood. I wonder what happened to it: I think we simply read it to pieces. Or we no longer needed it when the Irving Rosenthal-edited Grove Press came out (incorporating a few changes that I was able to spot immediately, that's how into Naked Lunch I was). Or maybe that copy still exists in Haselwood's "rich chaos" of an office in the Cotati-farmhouse he has inhabited for about 35 years.

So I read the article, skimmed it rather, noting additions I could have made, like that painting LaVigne did of Peter Orlovsky had another life after Ginsberg fell rather fatally for its subject: LaVigne left it with me and it hung on my wall at 1403 Gough for years, until I sent it to him strapped to the bed of a pickup headed for NYC where he supposedly had a buyer for it. He didn't. The next time I saw the painting was at the DeYoung Museum here in San Francisco in the travelling Beats show a few years ago. The painting is mythic, but a little overrated, (and I hope Bob doesn't ever read this): it captures what there was of Peter's boyish beauty to capture but it is really more LaVigne's salivating imagination of the ideal Narcissy, that neat pick curve of his cock. There is a strange foreshortening of space in the painting, not intentional I'm sure, that finally began to bug me. I was glad to see it go.

Back to synchronicity. I skimmed the article — it's very long and it's very good, mostly about Charley, an old friend of mine I haven't seen or corresponded with in years. I went on to read the comments posted (Karen is right about the two dayglos pink and orange of NOW; I wonder is that the Karen that turned Charley on to Dylan? I was there.) As I came to the end, reading the last comment, suddenly there appeared on my computer screen Charley's comment of Aug 30, 09 (today) at 6:17 p.m. How odd is that? How unlikely? That after years of separation our fingertips would suddenly touch in cyberspace?

Okay, you're not convinced. Try this for synchronicity. It's better.

In the summer of 1963 I shared 1403 Gough Street with Charles Plymell and Dave Haselwood and Neal Cassady and Anne Murphy and Maggie Harms and Justin Hein and Patricia Ross and Dave Moe and Marian Weston and other people I could name but I'd run out of space. As a matter of fact I did most of the fucking cooking. And cleaning. I was losing my mind. Dropping acid and out. Trying to write a novel. You wouldn't believe the chaos and energy and creativity – Charley writing poetry and reading it to whoever would listen, Justin painting sunburst murals in the hall, Ginsberg shaking his glory locks, Neal smacking Anne with a rubber hose. I thought life would be like that from then on, but, you know, it didn't really last much past the sixties.

It got to be too much for me, so me and my two lovers, Justin and Maggie, jumped in the Volks — it was Mag's car, she drove, with the baby on the top of a suitcase – and headed for Mexico. Bye, Charley, bye, it's your scene, take it! Sad though, because the previous winter we had all bonded – Charley, Dave, Maggie, Justin, me – we were the Fool Troop, we called ourselves, stoned and holy. So our little truncated caravan bounced up and down the Pacific coast of Mexico for a few weeks, we stuck a pin in the map and headed for it, run over by a Mexican truck that crushed the Volks, before we landed in the Merced Mercado in Mexico City where we were when we heard the news – eleven minutes after it happened – that Kennedy had been assassinated. We headed home, that was enough to put an end to the party. We drove up the middle of Mexico to some little border town in Arizona out in the middle of nowhere. We left the customs station and turned onto a US highway. A car was coming toward us, the first we met. As we got closer somebody waved – both cars stopped. Believe it or not, it was Charley, headed for New York with his girlfriend Anne Buchanan. The last person we said goodbye to when we left, the first person we see when we cross the border. Synchronicity. Charley went on to NY. We went on to SF.

I went back to 1403 Gough Street and lived there for about fifteen more years, a place where I sometimes find myself in dreams in the middle of the night. Oh yeah, when I was leaning into Charley's car out in the middle of the Arizona desert, I noticed a magazine lying on the backseat. It was NOW, but it had a different cover from the first, pinker, more garish, more day-glo, cheaper looking. I was glad I had the original issue.

POSTSCRIPT 2016

The Book of Friends ends here, right in the middle of things. The summer of 1963 that I shared the flat at 1403 Gough Street with Charley Plymell, Dave Haselwood, Neal Cassady, Ann Murphy, Justin Hein, Patricia Ross, Dave Moe, Marian Weston – I could name the others but I'd run out of space – was over for me. You wouldn't believe the chaos and energy and creativity contained within those walls – Charley ablaze writing poetry and reading it to whoever would listen, Justin painting sunburst murals in the hall, Ginsberg shaking his glory locks, Neal smacking Ann with a rubber hose: all against the backdrop of San Francisco where the hot masochism of the Beats was morphing into the cool sadism of Hip. I thought life would be like that from then on, but it didn't really last much past the sixties.

The scene got to be overcrowded for some of us, so Justin, Maggie with the baby Maia, and I jumped in the Volks — it was Mag's car, she drove, with the baby on the top of a suitcase – and headed for Mexico. Goodbye, Charley. It was sad though, because the previous winter we had all bonded – Charley, Dave, Maggie, Justin, me – we were the Fool Troop, as we called ourselves, stoned and holy. Our little truncated group bounced up and down the Pacific coast of Mexico for a few weeks -- we stuck a pin in the map and headed for it — run over by a Mexican truck that crushed the front of the Volks, before we landed in the Merced Mercado in Mexico City where we were when we heard the news – eleven minutes after it happened – that Kennedy had been assassinated. We headed home, that was enough to put an end to the party. We drove up the middle of Mexico to some little border town in Arizona out in the middle of nowhere. We left the customs station and turned onto a US highway. A car was coming toward us, the first we met. As we got closer somebody waved – both cars stopped. Believe it or not, it was Charley, headed for New York with his girl friend Anne Buchanan. The last person we said goodbye to when we left, the first person we see when we cross the border. There is much about time and place that is beyond our comprehension. Charley went on to NY. We went back to San Francisco.

    We returned to Gough Street where Maggie still had her place. The 1403 flat was just as Charley had left it. I hurriedly rented it with Haselwood and Justin from the Woodmansees, who owned the building. I lived there for about fifteen more years, mostly alone. Still today I sometimes find myself roaming its vast halls in dreams in the middle of the night.

    The Gough Street scene died slowly over a long period of time. People kept coming back to ring its bell, shaking their heads in bewilderment, as if they had misplaced something and perhaps had left it there. A bent profile in hood or bonnet, whispers a name, seeking news of others: Morgan and Lisa? Where? Most returned bedraggled, like wounded homing pigeons, messages garbled and skewed. I used to live here, I think, I did I know. Would you remember? Some mornings before I went to work Neal Cassady would materialize out of the laundry room off the back porch with a skinny waif of a chick (more often he was alone) and tap on the kitchen window, seeking sanctuary. The last time he came, early 1968, he was hungry. I was eating ice cream and gave him some. Ow, ow, ow! he cried in pain when the cold hit his empty stomach.

He confessed he was looking for speed. He was thin, worn -- gone in the face. The fabled Cassady beauty and energy were nowhere to be seen. He was any shriveled little man in wrinkled khakis looking for a corner to lie in. That was the last I saw of him. Not long afterward I heard he was dead in Mexico.

Above: Dave Moe and a friend in 2011, **Below:** Glen Todd and Dave Haselwood in 2011

Above: Charley Plymell holding up a copy of *The Last Times* in 2011,
Below: (Left to Right): Glenn Todd, Dave Haselwood, Charley Plymell and Bob Branaman in 1996 (Photo by Ralph Ackerman)
Following page: Charley Plymell and Joanne McClure in 2011

MY LAST DAYS AT THE GOUGH ST. FLAT
Charles Plymell

....that mysterious three-story Vic where the landlord lived in the bottom flat and was rarely seen. The School of Mortuary Science was in back of the back stairs that Neal came up in his last days, "gone in the face," said Glenn who lived there when we had THE party, high on LSD and "Panama Red." The door bell rang. I opened it. The Beat Generation was standing on the stoop. Inside, Dave Moe was dancing mad again. After a while Ginsberg came over to me and said, "I guess you're the one I'm supposed to meet." He talked in a smooth voice, a studied one as if learned in broadcasting school in Chicago where it was taught because of no accent. Glenn had a smooth West Texas voice like Bob Wills. Dave and Patricia lived down the way in trashed out old Fillmore houses ready to be torn down. Gough St. was on the slate & Glenn went to city officials and pitched a fit. He got a deal near where Mammy Pleasant pushed her banker husband off her mansion roof before the quake and planted the Eucalyptus trees still swaying a few years ago when Glenn took me past them. A voodoo-like group was standing on the plaque beneath them. "There's always something there every night," he said. Gough Street survived the razing wrecking ball, but they muddled it beyond recognition on purpose.

I rented the flat when some young Wichita meth-head burnouts left. I had no idea of the history of Ginsberg & Co, living there when he wrote & read Howl. Allen asked me if they could move in with me where he ostensibly could help Neal with his book. The Cassady-Ginsberg tenure began. We shared seven rooms at a hundred bucks a month. Ferlinghetti came over to help Ginsberg with Neal's writing of The First Third at the kitchen table as Neal rolled a joint from his shoebox full of weed. He talked too fast for them. I told them just to record him and transcribe it. I don't know what they did. I had a job downtown and rode my motorcycle to work, Neal on back of my new Honda cruiser motorcycle, the first import, with his railroad pocket watch, gauging our arrival time to the minute to his job where I dropped him off. Neal worked at a tire changing place on the corner of Van Ness. We went by the big drugstore on Van Ness and Market. Empty Cosanyl bottles were lined neatly along the curb. He worked so fast, the company had to let him go. All the rest of the help just stood and watched him.

Gough St, became a "beathive." Famous people came to visit. Junkies sent their old ladies to beg off Allen. Claude Pélieu and Mary Beach arrived with Mary's daughter, Pam, from France at Ferlinghetti's suggestion. Leary arrived sniffing out the Sandoz. I took Pam, who was under age to Mike's Pool Hall near City Lights Bookstore. Larry came with us as an establishment figure, so they never asked Pam's age. The old Italian men sat at the tables with red and white checkered table cloths and watch the pool players and put a quarter in the jukebox to play Enrico Caruso. Their minestrone was tops. The Salami Factory was next door. They made sandwiches with it and the San Francisco sourdough loaf. Pam and I later got married in Reno while baby sitting Richard White's puppy. It is our 50th Anniversary as I write this.

While riding down Market past the corner of Castro, I saw a girl standing queue waiting for the Mini bus. I thought Whaaa? I turned around and pulled up to her on my motorcycle, Brando fashion, and said "Hop on. I'm taking you home!" Ann Buchanan became a fixture at Gough St. Neal came in our room one day and yelled. "Turn on the TV, Charley, the president has been shot." Dark days followed. We had a Thanksgiving dinner to which all were invited. My sister, Betty and her old man, Frank came. And maybe a stranger from the street. The times became dark and depressing. Allen wrote his "Alone" poem that mentions us. Ann and I drove to Fairbanks, after Neal had check all our tires for the right air pressure and with his worried look, gave me some little white pills. We drove and drove.

Another uncannily mysterious event happened on our way to Tucson. Glenn, Maggie and her daughter Maia and Justin had all gone to Mexico in her VW bug and were returning west, then north to Frisco. Ann and I were headed to Tucson and points East in our

VW bug. "The two bugs and a roach" met in the middle of Arizona on Rt 66. I said, "Whaaa!!" And wheeled around. They had seen me waving and stopped! Ann and I continued on to Wichita and Moody's Skidrow Beanery and on to her folks house in Illinois then to NYC where I stayed on the Bowery with Crandal and Mary Joan Waid from my Wichita U. Days. Ann jumped ship and sought refuge at Warhol's factory. Some years later Glenn sent a tear sheet from London Times announcing her a leading off a video of Andy Warhol's Screen Test of "The Ten Most Beautiful." My long time friend, of the day and currently brought me a blow-up of her, shot from the screen test and rather apologetically acknowledged that: "He fell head over heels in love with her." I never saw her again, but heard last year at the All July party a punkette group, Luna made a song about her image in the video.

Redevelopment tore down the old section of the Fillmore where Dave & Patricia lived. Glenn would put his hand over his mouth and sighed when we'd try to image their happy married life there. A Chinaman had a corner grocery at Gough and Polk. He was upset about the redevelopment. "Where I flind another place for store"?

Glenn was the last man standing. I went by the address on a visit a few years ago and saw the horrible caul they had put over the top apartment...or something? Glenn had moved to his current place. Another weird thing was that when he was re-doing the basement there was the beginning of my "Glory Revolution" poem scrawled on the wall. There were several little holes bored into the wall. I thought it was listening posts for telephone or recorder jacks. Someone said it might have been for betting and bookmaking. I don't know.

Pam and I, after living in Lawrence Kansas, making the scene with S. Clay Wilson and John Fowler of Grist, returned to a Post St. ground level studio where we bought an old Multilith and ran the first ZAP. We also had naked parties there, in vogue at the time. Glenn ran naked from the Gough St. flat to our studio on Post St. to come to one of the parties.

I can't make these memories chronological "...as if a magic lantern threw a pattern on a screen" I think the poet said. They are like a kaleidoscope. It may have been the Sandoz, the Owsley, the pure Mescaline, the shoebox of Panama Red. The memories come in bits. Like I lived in a pad in 1962 two houses up on Ashbury off Haight in a pleasant Russian neighborhood. I woke up one morning thinking I heard Ravi Shankar and saw Jerry Garcia and others crowding the little old Russian ladies off the sidewalk. The street filled up with hippies. Richard Brautigan and I sat in a café near Stanyan. The streets were shoulder to shoulder with the new hippies. He became one. I took Allen up there one time and he was puzzled at the scene trying to get "Haight" spelled right, so John Ashbery in NYC wouldn't think he was starting a Hate-Ashbury movement. I characterize THE party as one where the Beats met the Hippies.

Glenn Todd was born in Archer City, Texas, in 1930. After high school he served in the United States Army in Texas. He studied English Literature at Wichita State University and did graduate work the University of California at Berkeley. Beginning in 1964 he worked as a printer for the San Francisco fine printers and publishers Andrew Hoyem, Grabhorn-Hoyem, and Arion Press, where he became an editor and wrote introductions to some of its publications. He was the author of a monograph on the history of poems written in graphic arrangements for Shaped Poetry and introductory essays to The Temple of Flora, The Captivity Narrative of Hannah Duston, and Eureka by Edgar Allan Poe. After his retirement in 1995, he began writing fiction. Todd is working on a novel entitled "Smooch".

COLOPHON

The Book of Friends was published by Bottle of Smoke Press in January 2017. Designed by Bill Roberts in the hamlet of Wallkill, NY. The text is set in 12 point Adobe Caslon Pro.

www.ingramcontent.com/pod-product-compliance
Lightning Source LLC
Chambersburg PA
CBHW051701040426
42446CB00009B/1243